RAPIDITÀ ESATT-
EZZA MOLTE-
PLICITÀ
VISIBILITÀ
ITALO CALVINO.

Mandragora s.r.l.
via Capo di Mondo 61
50136 Firenze
www.mandragora.it

Printed in Italy
isbn 978-88-7461-682-4

ANDREW MORE O'CONNOR

A Tuscan Résumé

Mandragora

June 30 2010.
ROME .VIA FIAMINA

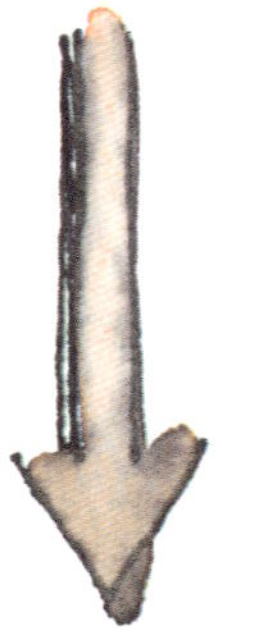

Contents

Preface

In Father Andrew O'Connor's 'Tuscan Résumé', the saying 'Beauty is in the eye of the beholder' expands to 'Beauty is in the eye and heart of the beholder'. Father Andrew, an artist and priest of the Archdiocese of New York, recounts his impressions during a peripatetic retreat in Tuscany some years ago, under the guidance of a priest who is also an art historian – myself. My hope was to help my listeners open to the spiritual as well as aesthetic beauty of the buildings, sculptures and paintings seen together, and Father Andrew's text tells me that something of this sort happened, at least in his case. His enthusiasm reflects my own, and since the Greek sources of that English word, 'enthusiasm', regard God's presence in human hearts, we may say that 'Tuscan Résumé' is an 'inspired' work – a 21st-century response to the same Spirit who touched the architects and artists whose masterpieces Father Andrew describes: the 'Creator Spiritus' to whom Christians sing at Pentecost. Readers of this short but moving account will, I think – like me – exclaim: 'Hallelujah', 'Praise the Lord'!

Msgr. Timothy Verdon

Director, Cathedral Museum, Florence, Italy

MUSEO DELL'OPERA DEL DUOMO

Forward

Fifty years ago, the Southern poet Allen Tate remarked in an important essay on the symbolic imagination that America is as dependent on a diminished Europe as ancient Rome was on a diminished Greece. What he meant was that the survival and flourishing of our most important social institutions, including the Church, demand of us an on-going and genuinely engaged reflection with the past. To ignore our deep human and institutional need for engaged reflection is to risk losing that unique recipe that is the western tradition. It is the proverbial salt and yeast in the dough. Priests too are called to engaged reflection. Specifically, we are required by canon law to take an annual week of study, which we rarely do, for our renewal and for the renewal of the Church. At the invitation and urging of our New York Archbishop Timothy Dolan we decided we needed to engage the foundational western church and starting July 1st, 2010, twenty-two priests of the Archdiocese of New York – myself included – traveled to Italy for a ten-day term of study in Tuscany and Venice. We were honored to have as our director the esteemed Reverend Doctor Monsignor Timothy Verdon, Canon of the Diocese of Florence, and a Yale-trained American art historian. What follows is a résumé of our day-to-day encounter with our western roots through the history, art, culture, and theology of Catholic Italy. This is a pilgrimage of beauty and a feast of history. Beyond a summary of how we spent our week of study in Tuscany and Venice, is a résumé of sorts that suggests how we as priests could employ art as a handmaiden to theology and the sacramental life, as if art came to your door one day and gave you a Tuscan (and Venetian) résumé in search of employment in the life of the Church.

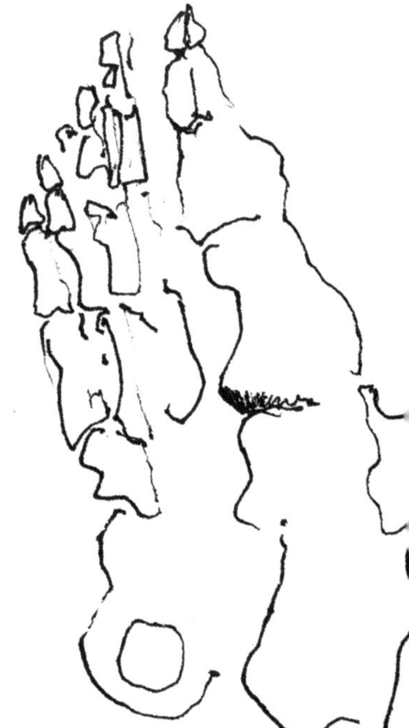

Introduction

Thomas a Becket, Bishop and Martyr. December 29, 2023 Commemoration. Friday noon mass at Cabrini. I had the mass as a left-over obligation since returning from Italy on November 15. Fr. Tom Madden the pastor of St. Peter's in Haverstraw fell just before Christmas. I was sent to help. He was convalescing in the Cardinal Egan Residence in Riverdale in the Bronx. I came to visit after the mass, it is a short drive from Inwood over Spuyten Duyvil. The Visitation Sisters's convent is a stone fortress on the palisades over the Hudson. It is the same campus I came to in January 1990 when I entered the seminary after leaving Dallas and after my sister Molly's wedding.

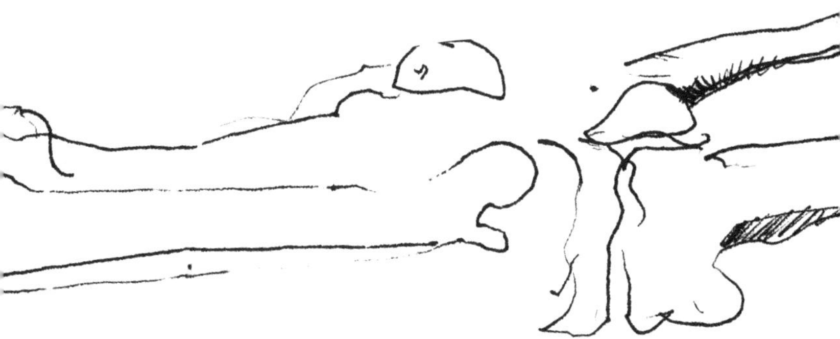

'If we who are called bishops desire to understand the meaning of our calling and to be worthy of it, we must strive to keep our eyes on him whom God appointed high priest forever, and to follow in his footsteps'. From a letter by St Thomas a Becket, Bishop.

Fr. Ed Barry stepped into the room where I sat with Fr. Tom Madden. 'Most people take out cameras when they travel, this guy takes out a book and draws a picture'. He says that out of the blue. I haven't seen him much in the 14 years since we went to Tuscany together.

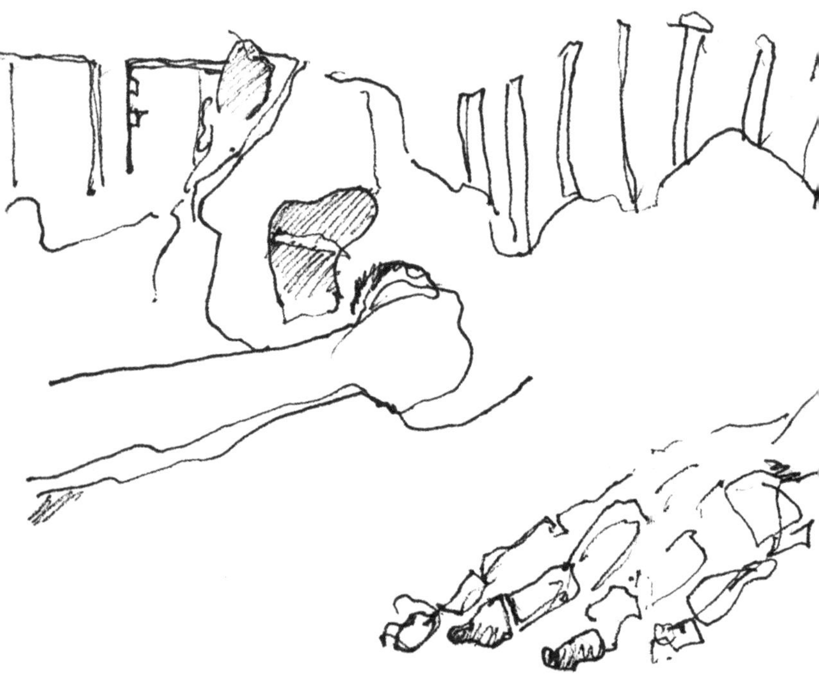

– Good drawings.

– I am publishing a book on it called *A Tuscan Résumé.*

– I remember I bought a liter and a half of bourbon in the airport heading there. Whatever made me do that. And it was gone. We were in the residence there. Where was it?

– La Verna. At the foot of the mountain. Stigmata of St Francis. Walter Kenny's raked hat.

– I remember. Walter always had such style.

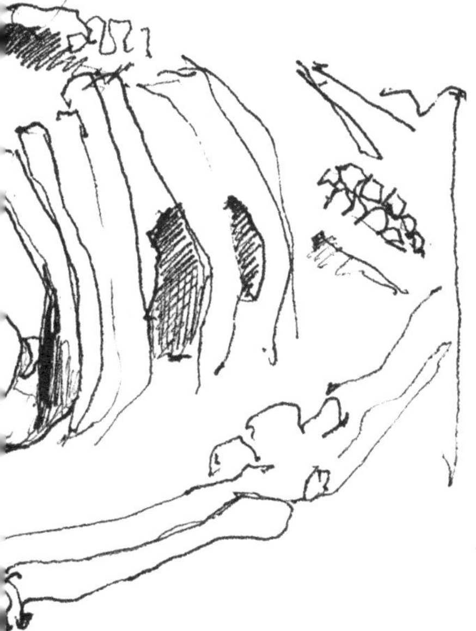

We do like to take pictures. I prefer to draw and to write and to remember. I offer this book in appreciation to Cardinal Dolan who sponsored this retreat to Tuscany, in 2010, less than a year after being made Archbishop of New York, and to the priests who came on the trip. The content is a résumé, which is greater than a reminiscence: it is returning to where we have been for the sake of resuming where we left off. The medium is central to the work. A wider audience than priests may wish to take note. The act of the journal is the subject.

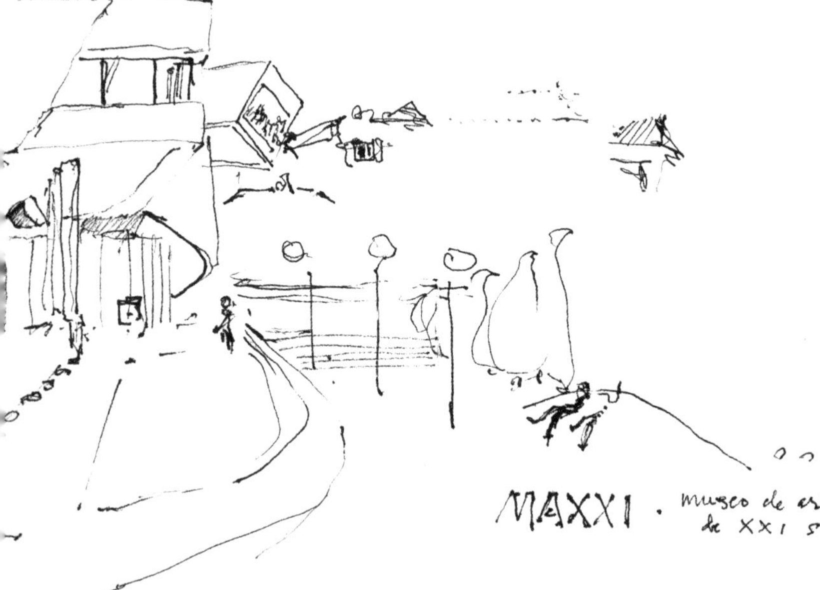

Whether drawings or photos, the pictures we take are nothing compared with those we might like to take or are naturally absorbing. Martin Heidegger points out how Being (*Sein* and *Dasein*, 'to be there') pulses with the desiderata of meaning in images and in words. Most are lost. Our sleep is inhabited with rivers of images. When we wake we would like to return to them. Photography is easy now. It is not a luxury anymore. It chronicles and edits, though it does not edit itself. In that regard it is an unassailable witness that does not shut up

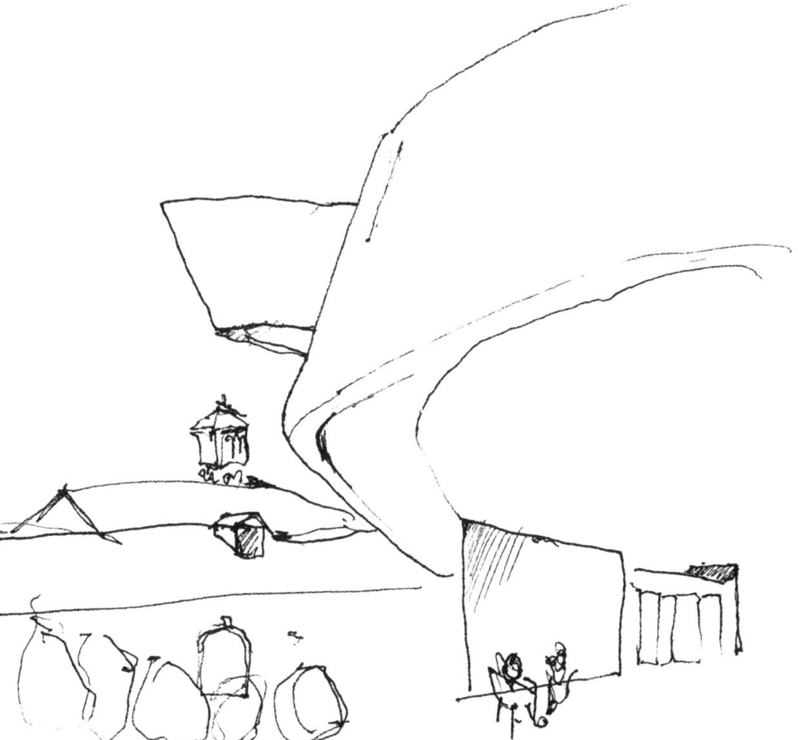

on the witness stand. The witness has said too much and no one is listening anymore. It deprives us of our recollection. Generally, photos grow untamed like weeds. When we want them to mean something intended or unintended, however, it is time to weed. Would you go to Tuscany without a phone to photograph or to FaceTime or to Instagram? *A Tuscan Résumé* may inspire you to take the road less traveled. When forced to compare other people's photos with our own, ours may wither and fade. Conversely, we might perceive that there is a characteristic personality to our photos. I would hope both would happen. I would suggest foregoing the photo for a time and trying to draw instead will enhance seeing. Things fading away help us see. 'Back out of all this now too much for us, / back in a time made simple by the loss / of detail, burned, dissolved and broken off / like graveyard marble sculpture in the weather' begins Robert Frost in his 1947 poem *Directive.* It was a post-war command to ascend by stepping away from too much detail. To draw a picture rather than to take a picture is the work of getting free from what is 'all of this too much for us'. All of our senses crave definition. When you draw, especially when you draw on the move, you have to choose what can define. In fact, you are drawn into what is before you. You anchor yourself from the restless need to depart. You become still. You are conscious of the birds, the stray conversations, the forgiving perfumes of the crushed path underfoot.

The drawings, notes and subsequent essay *A Tuscan Résumé* were made fresh fourteen years ago. Thanks to Monsignor Timothy Verdon who offered to read it October 2023 in Florence. He saw this trinity as a *factum est.* He suggested making the first paragraph a forward and kindly wrote the preface.

Let it serve as a guide to imitate as well as the worthy subject of a journey through Tuscany led by Monsignor Timothy Verdon. Christianity is a cosmopolitan religion. It is flowing with images that have suffered iconoclasts, both vulgar and humanist. When we met after mass one Sunday last October, Monsignor Verdon mentioned that priests after Vatican II rarely preach the literalness of the Annunciation. The angel Gabriel appeared to Mary. Monks in monasteries and contemplatives in the church, he noted, are comfortable with abstract art on the subject. The people deserve something concrete because it was concrete. The angel was really in the room. Mary really spoke with the angel. Later in October I visited the Uffizi and entered the crowded room where Leonardo da Vinci's *Annunciation* commands the center of the side wall. I am the fifth of nine and my mother had a small copy of that *Annunciation* in the living room. We were playing football inside the house forbidden by my mother. Did the picture fall? I just remember seeing it as precious from then on. A crowd of Americans gathered in front of the painting. The guide said that for Leonardo the shadow unfolding before the kneeling angel was a sign of his new humanistic thinking. He was moving away from the superstition of religion. The guide offered the proof that in Catholic theology angels do not have bodies and artists would not depict angels with shadows. True, angels would not be depicted with shadows. True, they are incorporeal creatures of light. 'Poppycock!' I thought. Angels are incorporeal but this one cast a shadow. 'The power of the Holy Spirit will overshadow you' (Luke 1:35). Leonardo had a clear subject and a commission he was fulfilling. That is no ordinary shadow. The shadow is strong and directed toward the Virgin Mary. The virgin conceived. There is no strong light behind the angel, no squinting from Mary. The other shadows in the painting are diffused and have a different angle. I wondered how many others also doubted what the guide said.

Was it exceptional that I was able to see that and the crowd could not? How could a visionary like Leonardo not help you to see? For me drawing and knowing are instinctual. I find I need to draw people from life rather than from a photo. The small movements sitting still also define. By extention, *A Tuscan Résumé* may be savoring the levels of meaning of the 'word made flesh'. In Arezzo's Basilica of San Francesco, in the frescoes of Piero della Francesca, made famous in the midair illumination with a flare in the film *The English Patient*, dying Adam reclines with his mouth open. His son Seth plants a sprig of the tree of the knowledge of good and evil into his mouth. It will grow into the wood of the true cross. A fragment of the body of Christ is the whole body of Christ; these fragments of images are potent and alive.

I thank Monsignor Verdon for graciously receiving me and allowing me to comment on his retreat. He gave us the fullest version. By coincidence he was an early and important element in my own vocation animated by my love of the arts. I was in high school when my mother arranged for me to attend 'Monasticism and the Arts' at the Yale Divinity School. Monsignor Verdon organized that symposium. For the publication of this book he introduced me to Dr. Mario Curia of the publishing house Mandragora, Firenze. Dr. Curia has embraced this book. Some years ago Laura Inghirami came to St Mary's while I was pastor there. She was surprised that I knew and loved Sansepolcro in eastern Tuscany. She has been an interceding angel. I thank her and her gracious family for opening so many doors for me and successively welcoming my own family, including the young men from St Mary on the Lower East Side who were part of our Rome program. By extention, I must thank Giuseppe Del Barra of the Sbandieratori di Sansepolcro as well as Paul Contini at San Martino Val d'Afra, for welcoming me in Sansepolcro. One can never be just a tourist with a vocation in Christ. I have grown as an artist through their help past, present and future in pursuing affresco and the study of Piero della Francesca. Massimiliano Pozzi and family gave me a home and a church over Lake Como where they live to give me holy refuge. They interceded with many connections and lent me a Porsche to drive around Italy and make my appointments. I thank Monsignor Artie Mastrolia for the title of *A Tuscan Résumé.* It was the fruit of our conversations at the time, our visit to Torcello and his durable and wise friendship.

A few kilometers outside of Sansepolcro, in Monterchi, Piero della Francesca's *Madonna del Parto* places her finger between the folds of her dress to reveal her pregnancy. Two angels half her size pull back the curtains of a small room where she alone inhabits the space. She gazes beyond the viewer, as in many Renaissance paintings. She possesses queenly patience. What does she see? What do we see? Something revealed and yet still hidden. From 2013 to 2023 I have had the opportunity to pastor the parish of St Mary in Lower Manhattan on Grand Street. Instead of rushing to finish all that needs to be done, I took the time to set in motion the spirituality of looking beyond the viewer. Peter Pisani, a carpenter for whom I prayed to St Joseph one night in 2013, arrived the next day looking for a job. Among our projects were new doors for the church. We built them ourselves out of solid mahogany, renting a pickup truck each time we could afford more wood and running up to the Bronx, to Rosenweig's to grade and weigh each plank. The doors took three years to cure on their hinges. Seepage of once new wood turned gray in the blasts of New York weather. We took them down, and sanded and sealed them. With the silversmith Chris Knight in Sheffield in the U.K., we fashioned laser cut cladding in bronze to sheath the doors with honeycomb and a horizon of crosses. The doors are titled: *Lux Mundi,* Light of the World. People wonder if the doors are old or new? The reaction continues inside the church. It is old and it is new. Such is the mystery of a pregnant virgin. May the account of this retreat for priests from the Archdiocese of New York in 2010 invite you to the transcendent grace of always beginning. *Semper incepit.*

Reverend Andrew More O'Connor
St Peter's and St Mary's
115 Broadway
Haverstraw, New York

July 2. 2010.

Fr. Timothy Verdun. at Pastor Angelicus in Vertsa Chiusa

shift from Antique world of citys 5c - 6c → to fuedal system. in the germanic tribal agglomerations. Charlemagne crowned on Christmas Day 900. new Christian Collaboration in the Holy Roman Empire. Conti Guidi - ruled Tuscany from Lucca. Redevelopment of cities - sheep fairs of florence + weaving wool. export wool and buy futures + invent a banking system with letters of credit. Growth of great wealth - 11th + 12th c. new autonomous City States.

11 June 1229 Campoldino. battle

July 2nd, Friday. Poppi

In a classroom at Pastor Angelicus, a chalet-styled retreat center at the foot of the looming sanctuary of St Francis in La Verna in Eastern Tuscany, Monsignor Verdon opened with a lecture on the 'shift from the antique world of cities in the fifth and sixth centuries A.D. to a feudal system in the Germanic tribal agglomerations'. His point that civilization can and did regress set the stage for the dramatic way in which civilization was reborn along with the rise of the merchant class in the nearby cities. Following the lecture we took a bus to the church of Pieve di Romena in the nearby valley of Poppi. The building embodies the Romanesque style in its haphazard memory of Roman grandeur. Its sturdy rounded apse and cave-like slits for windows, hand built by itinerant masons, sit alone in wheat fields. It is called 'Pieve' as a corruption of 'plebs' or people. The isolation of the valley shielded the local people from the barbarians. There was no more indoor plumbing or the sanitation that the Romans took for granted, but what emerged was a Christian faith that blended with local traditions that the church absorbed and used to help fortify the security of a class system. Allegiance to the church and the local fiefdom was rewarded with protection and the blessing of peace. The powerful union of the caste system of the fiefs was embodied in the term

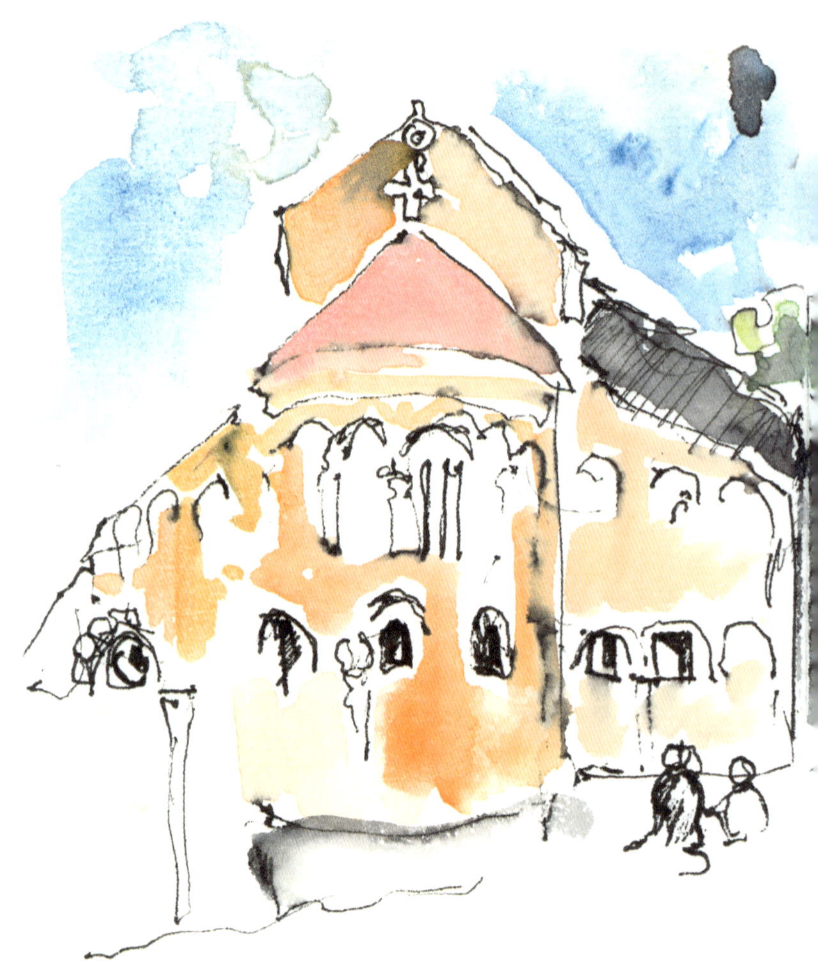

"DON" priest / lord.

PIEVE DE ROMENA - PLEBS or Popo

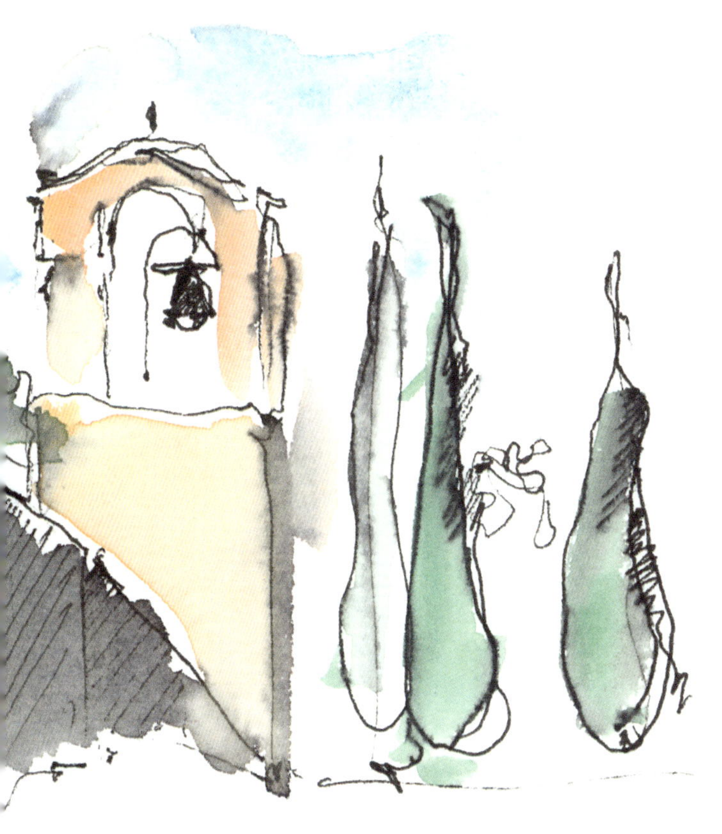

Bps of FIESOLE were imperial nobles
CIVIL IMPLICATIONS FOR THIS rural
parish. picked up the pieces of
Roman Civilization. Pievano – local
Zenobius – Bp. elevated headpriest.
DIOSESE OF FIESOLE 11 AM

for the parish priest still used today in Italy: 'Don'. The parish priest, often rudimentarily educated, was also a Lord ('Don' is from Dominus or Lord). As the papacy filled the empty throne of the emperor in the centuries before Charlemagne's crowning as Holy Roman Emperor on Christmas Day 800 A.D., so too did local Dons create an aristocracy. Following Charlemagne, this feudal power was more clearly in the hands of non-clerical Lords, who in this valley occupied an even higher land than the Church.

The church's thick walls and thin windows make the interior unchangeably cool. We file down into the undercroft to see the outline of an original foundation. Monsignor Verdon points out the egg and dart carving of the Roman style. Other carvings look Celtic with their concentric circles. We step out into the courtyard in front of the church under some olive trees. The air has an unnamable and sublime flower on it. Half of the priests have straw hats. Walter Kenny's has a rake to it. He looks like a real 'Don' and sits against the enclosing wall glancing.

In the distance from the church a fortified hill shows the shadowed outline of a tower. The town hall/castle of Poppi is our next destination and once up on the bridge entering the castle it is clear that the power to dominate must have come along with the bird's eye view. In the fields below the first battle between the

celtic decoration.

cap. frag
in under
Grots - early
apse.

egg + dart
Roman

crossed keys
of St. Peter

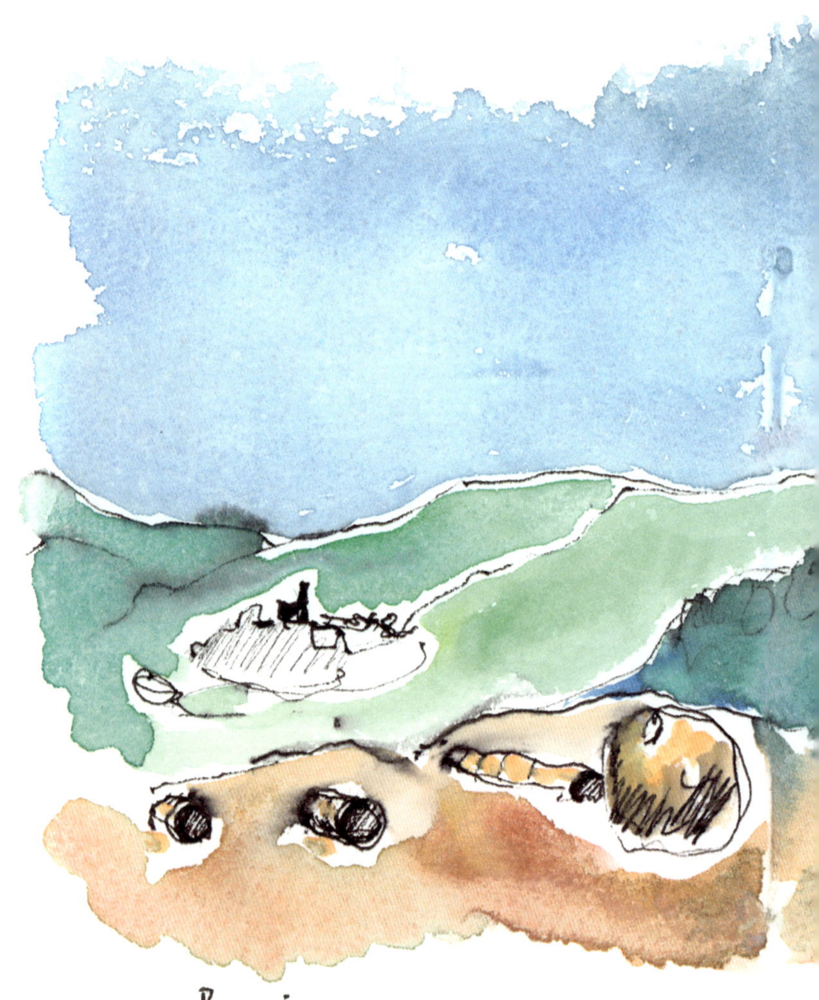

Poppi - CASTLE OF GUIDI COUNT

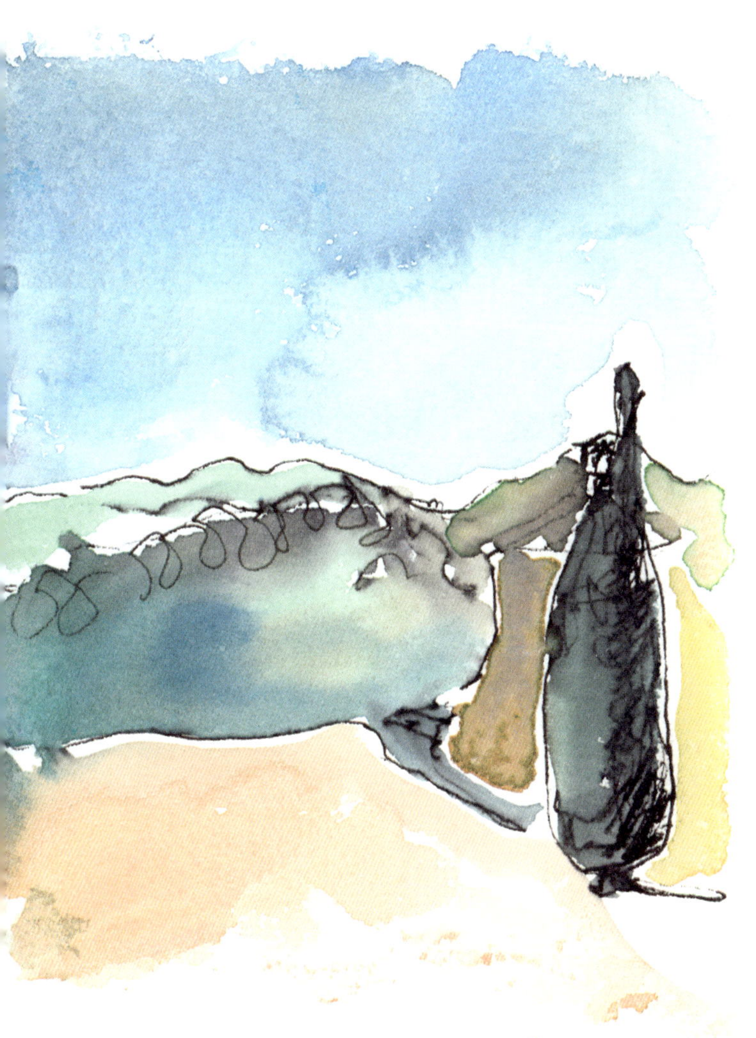

NTS. 11:10 AM. JULY 2, 2010

Aug. of Cant
Speaks of
English customs
Grey says "if
not opposed
absorb."

detail of
Capitol.

original
church dates
back to Charlemagne.

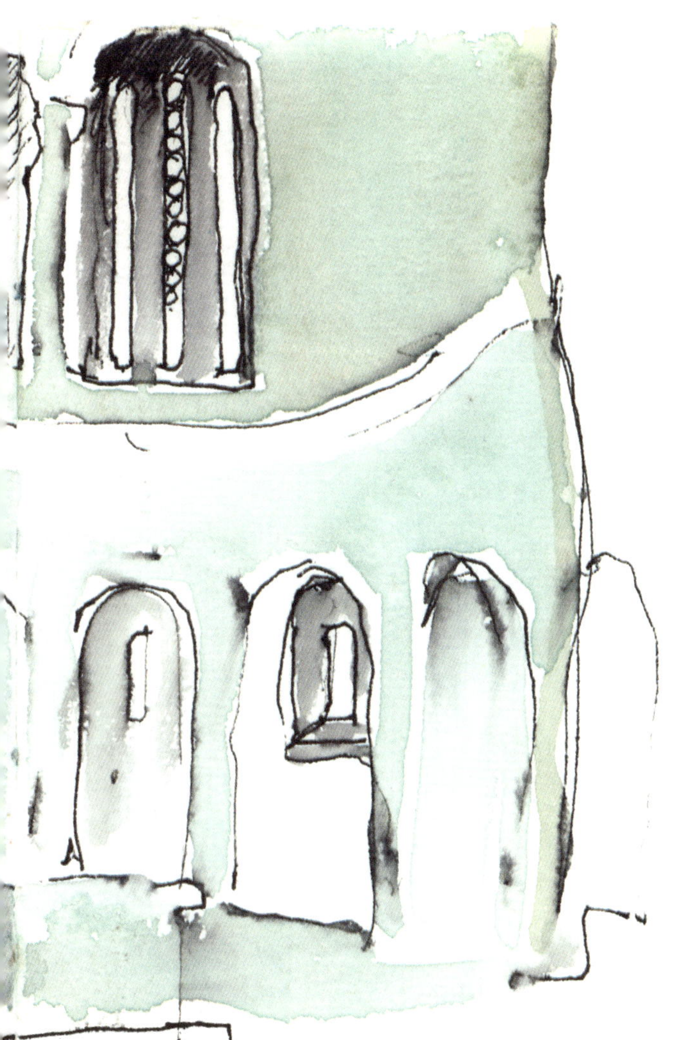

IN THE YEAR OF FAMINE 1152
interior. MEMORY OF ROMAN.
GRANDEUR – ~POPE surrogate emperor

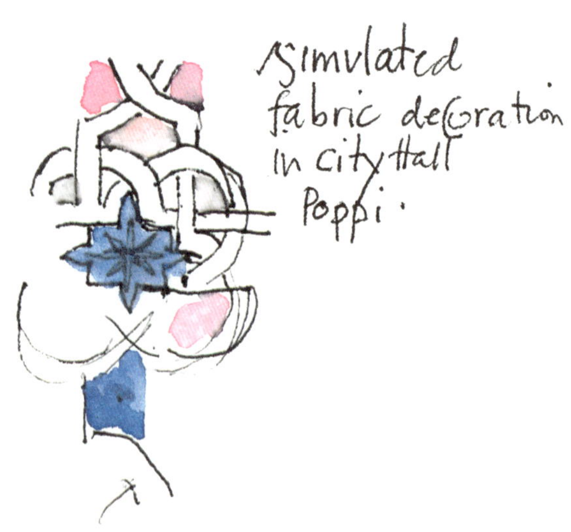

pro-emperor Ghibellines and the pro-civitas Guelphs was fought in 1250. The local lords, Ghibellines, won against the Guelph forces of the rising merchant class, the winnings of which were invested in the fortification. A private chapel off the secluded and relatively plain royal apartments is lavished with early frescoes. These paintings have the beginnings of the realism in that Tuscan style that strongly suggest the underpinnings of the Renaissance. The walls fall a hundred feet out the windows and are very strong, but not invincible to the will to win. The taxation and legal impunity that came with inherited titles eventually contributed to the crumbling of feudal authority as the wool traders of Florence developed modern financial tools like a letter of credit and the selling of futures and grew accustomed to the ease of lucrative contractual relationships.

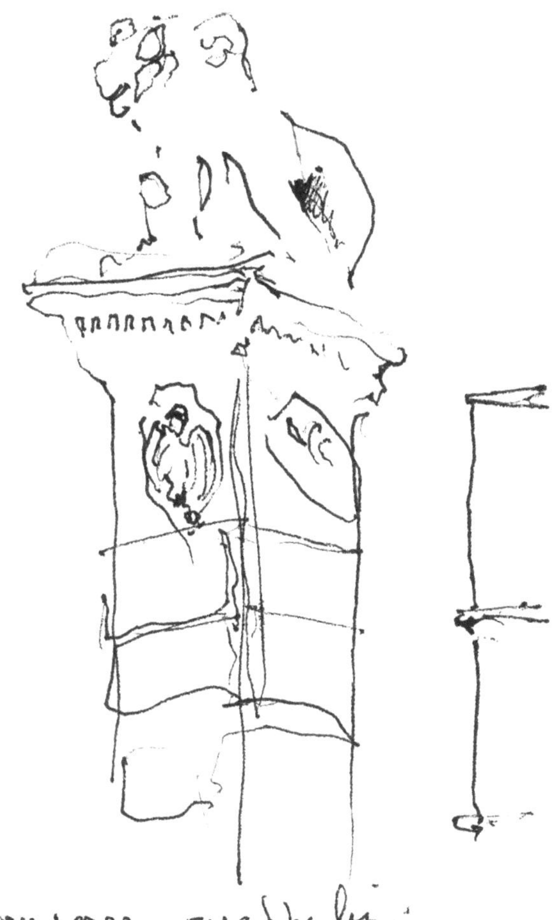

pro emperor guebbelin·

pro civitas. guelph. 1250 built

town hall Bardello. 1260 siena

vmonte Perdi. defeated Florence.

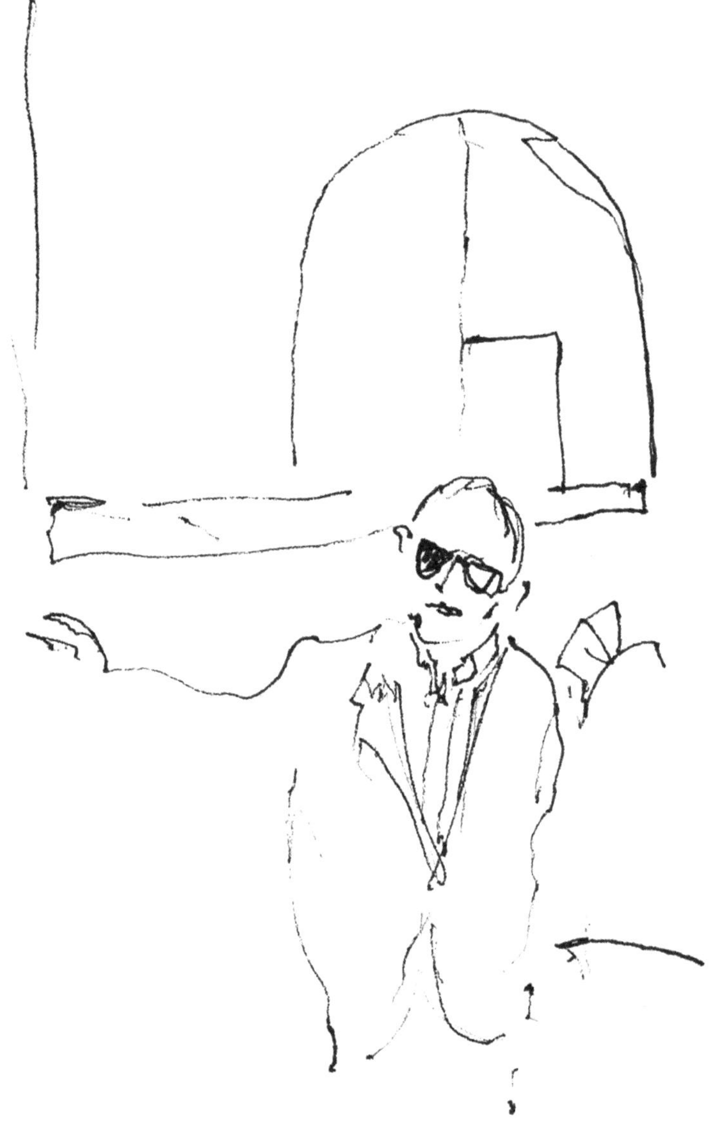

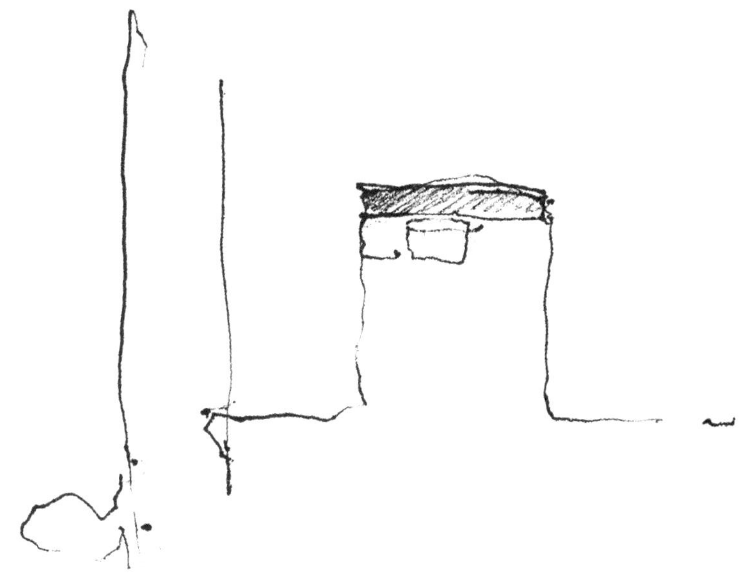

Castle of Poppi -

11 June. 1289 - column of battle.

Battle. guelphs won. with political vision of merchant, bankers & artisans created subsequent Splendor. Campaldino

Dante was 24. Guelph freedom fighter

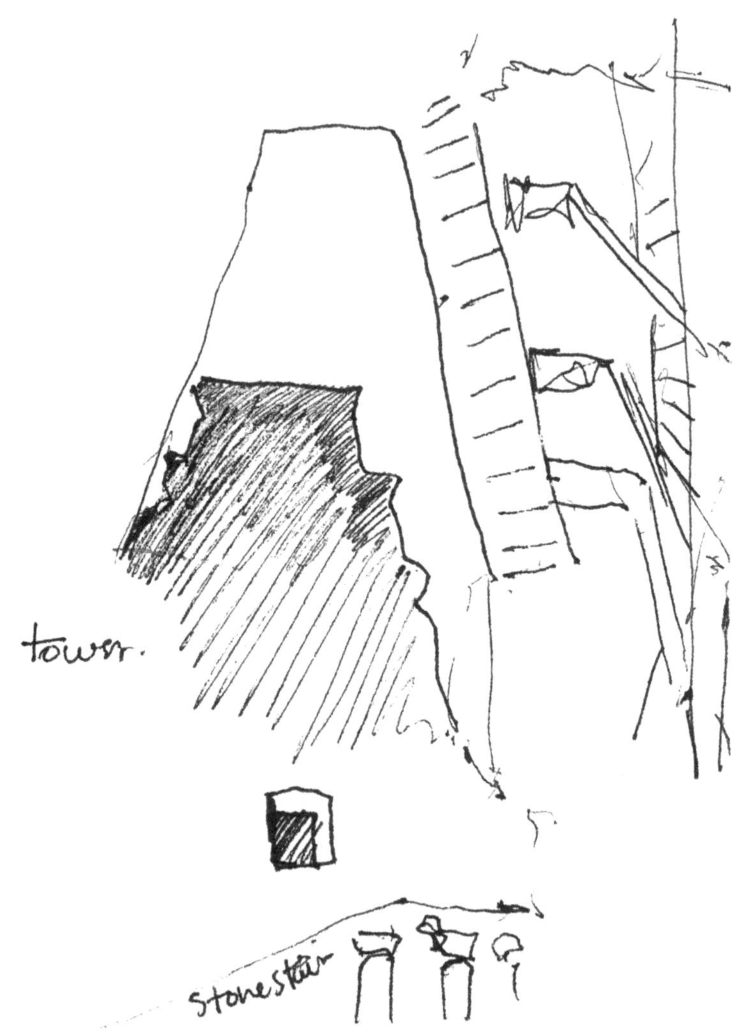
tower.
stonestair

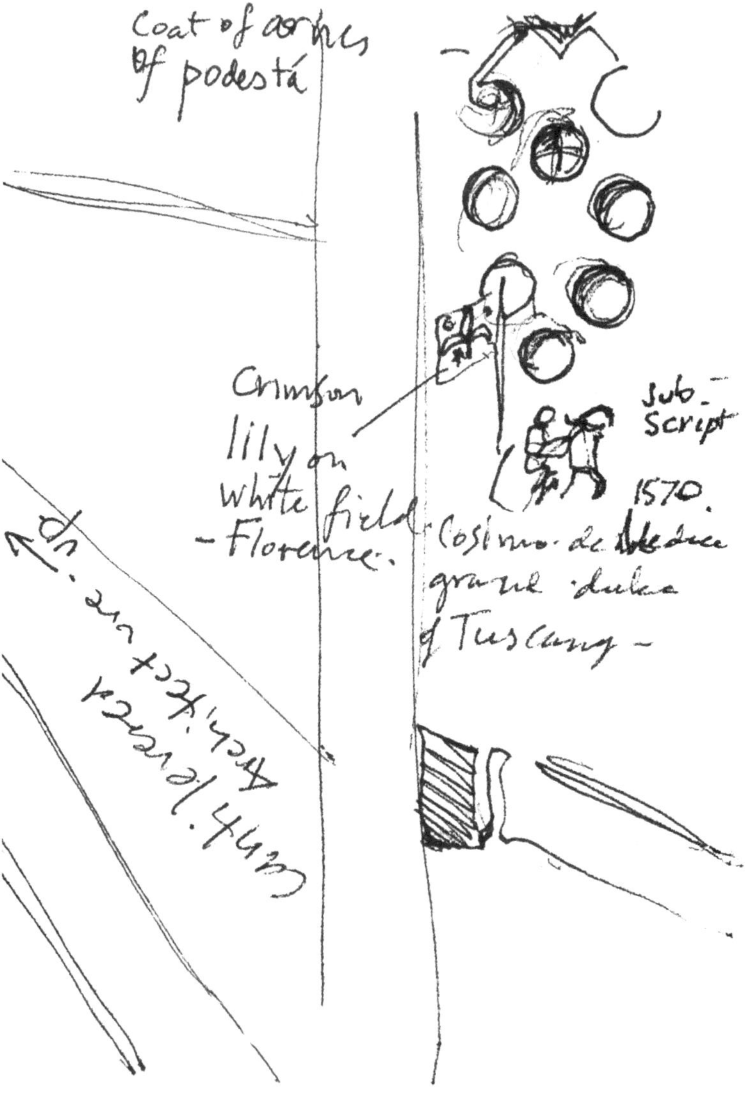

Coat of arms
of podestá

Crimson
lily on
white field
– Florence.

Sub-
Script

1570.

Cosimo de Medici
grand duke
of Tuscany –

with lower
architecture up

2nd or 3rd Son could live
in decorative style. put into
Church and given privilege
here in this Country tower.
They could become abbotts –
of Benedictines. or chaplain of
Household.

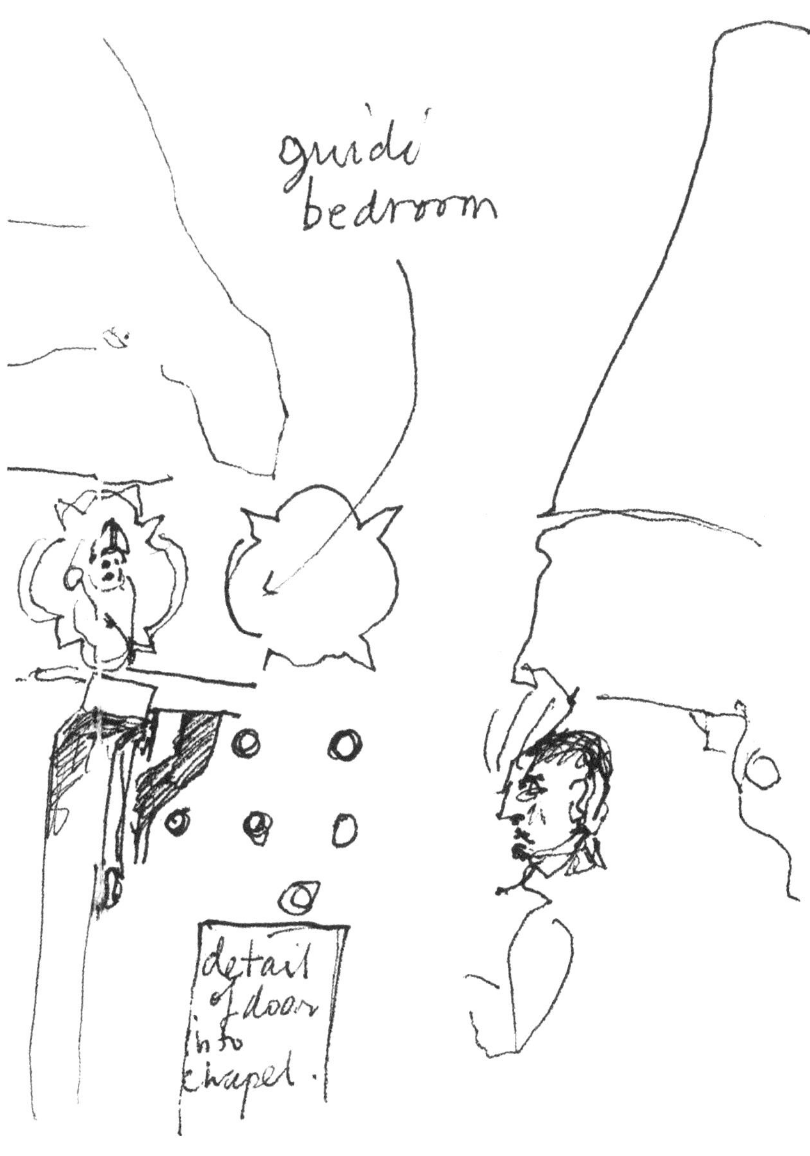
guidi
bedroom
detail
of door
into
chapel.

On June 11th, 1289 a third battle was fought in the fields of Campaldino. A miniature of that decisive battle is poised on a table in the castle. The Guelphs carry the flag of the crimson lily on a white field, the symbol of Florence. They are an all-volunteer force. The Ghibellines, in contrast, fight with hired hands and lose and the losers became slaves. On the facing wall hangs a painting of the 24-year-old Dante Alighieri who fought on the winning side in the battle. Already a popular poet of the sonnets of *Vita nova* in 11 years he will be exiled permanently from the city he fought for while on a diplomatic mission to nearby Arezzo. The dates and political divisions reveal what a condensed period of turmoil this was. For instance, St Francis died at the age of 44 only 39 years before Dante was born, himself the son of a wool merchant.

I don't know if they broke for lunch during battle but we did. What can Americans learn from life in Italy: pace yourself. After lunch we drove to Camaldoli, higher in the mountains than even La Verna and cool even in the afternoon sun. Fr. Sorgie reminds us that Cardinal O'Connor came here for retreats. The crimson lily of Florence appears again in the wrought iron that separates us from a small peaked range of eremitic huts that fade into the heavy forest. The Medicis too in all their worldliness came here for retreat. Sons were sent to be monks and equals to the most common man.

Comoldoli
4:30 pm. 2.10..
lavra hermits
Semi eremitic
life of St. Romuald

dreams of white robes
climbing to heaven 1020.

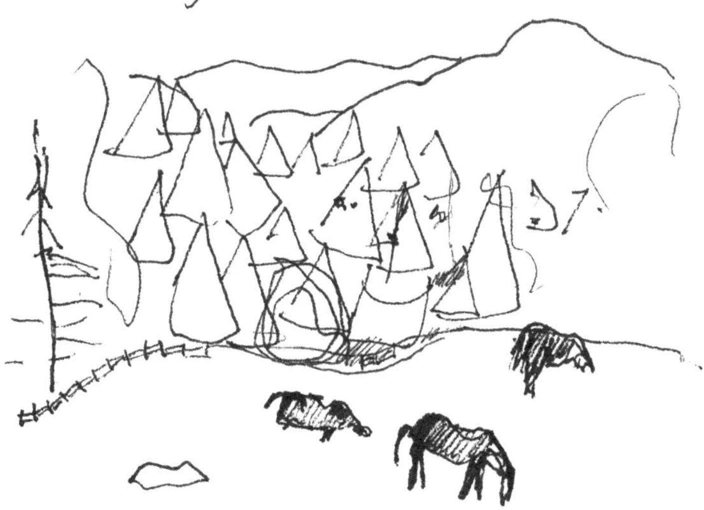

tree trunks of monks timber busines.

St Romuald had a vision in 1020 A.D. of white robes climbing into heaven here and created the secret source of good government: the chapter room. In this case the chapter room, where monks confess faults to each other humbly, has an inlaid floor in a honey-colored wood in beveled squares. Here is something we don't have in America that we desperately need: sacred ground in the form of a simple and beautiful floor. Our sacred floors invariably have pews bolted in. A good hand-made open floor in a sacred space would teach us to tread lightly on each other's dreams. Camaldoli have the soul to make things. Lumber was their stocking trade and prized in Florence. Today they make a range of goods from liquor to shampoo beautifully and simply done in their tradition that helps support the monastery.

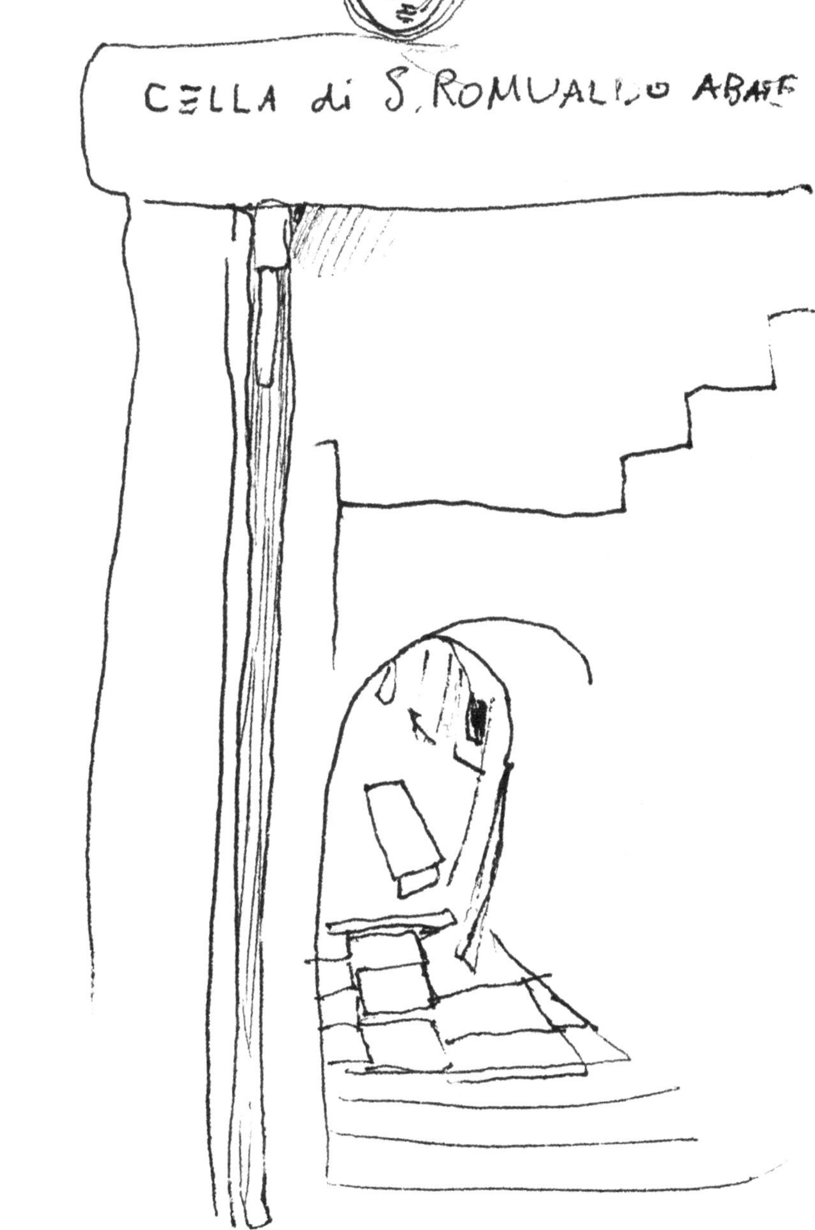
CELLA di S. ROMUALDO ABATE

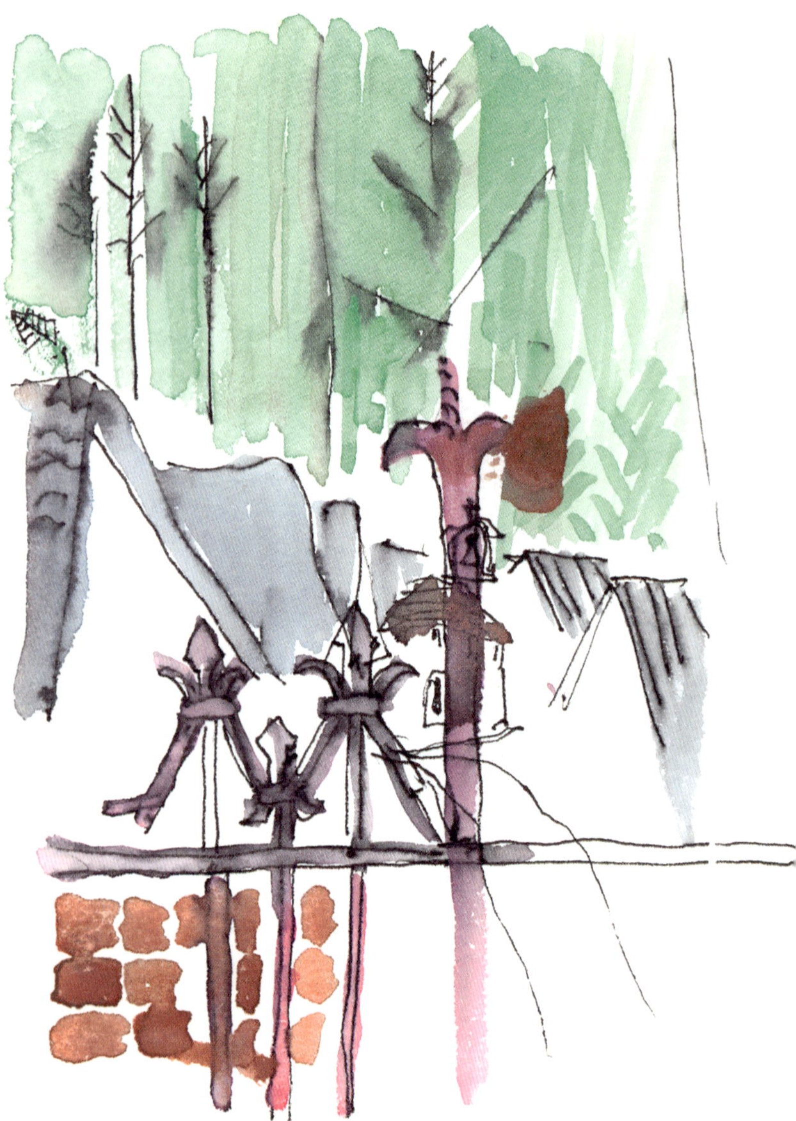

July 3rd, Saturday. La Verna

Having the monastic tradition in mind primed us for the next morning's visit to the Sanctuary of La Verna and an introduction to St Francis, superstar saint. Monsignor Verdon was freed up to meet us for a lecture in the morning. Half of us chose to hike up through the sacred woods including 83 year old Fr. Louis Mazza. Another thing we can learn from the Italians is to keep gleaning the woods for good firewood for pizza. Not only do the woods still look as good as in the Bellini painting in the Frick, but pizza in wood-fired ovens is sublime. Ascending drenches us in green, in silence, and in vigor. A large tumbling piazza in rough stone unfolds at the summit, but not after the misdirection of low arched tunnels and the hips of chapels. A telephone-pole high cross impales the stone's edge where a brass button can be pushed to spout spring water. After a few handfuls of water the vista of the country below suggests how Graymoor got it right. The mountain was the gift of Count Orlando Catani in 1215, an otherwise useless property as sometimes is the case in gifts from the wealthy. The 'Foreste Sacre' surrounds the whole sanctuary. There are many approaches as I found out from several runs in the subsequent days. If you are given to finding God in nature, you will find Him here in abundance. Beware, the spirituality of this place is intoxicating.

Francis was the right person to the give the mountain to. His whole being needed it and he came back to it four times more in the final 13 years of his life. He was not a monk, but he embodied the need to blend the two worlds. There had been a centuries-long drought of saints and his appearance really shook the world. To be sure, Pope Innocent III stands in the background as a model of how to let God's work be done. Another Pope may have easily denied granting a charter to Francis. In the imagination of Francis, which in Tuscany in this time meant the quest for the real and not escape from it, Christ mystically emerges out of true humility. Monsignor Verdon leads us along a long outer hall of mediocre frescoes of scenes from the life of Francis. The hall narrows and a door, seemingly entering into through one of the paintings, opens to a rustic courtyard. The uneven steps lead down to a damp cave, Francis' rock bed. We stop and visit in turns. The thrust of a rock inches from where his chest would have been make the weight suspended in the rock feel like the rest a head might have between an anvil and a hanging hammer. It is not likely he ever got much sleep there. Brother falcon came and Francis rose and went out onto the ledge of his vision of the seraphim which opened the wounds of Christ for him and in him. Another time the devil tempted him there on the ledge with the valley below, pulling him off the ledge. God drew him back. Turning back down the same hall the stories unfold in the accordion book of frescoes: the wolf at Gubbio and conversation

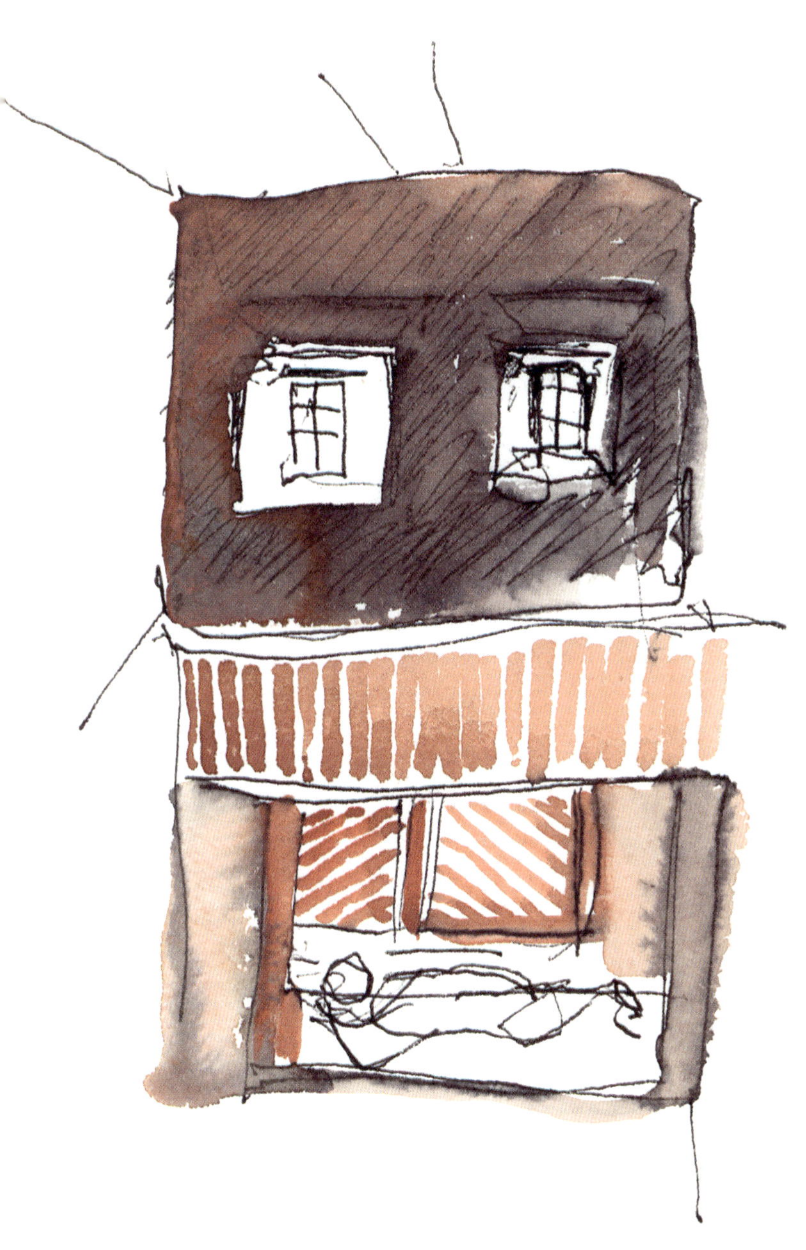

1215 Count Orlando Cotani
donated the mountain La Verna
after Frances's spoke of Christ:
mystical prayer in the midst
of nature and charismatic
Communion with god drew
Frances four times more in
the final 13 years of his life.
"Around the feast of the
Exaltation the Cross" in 1226.
- open gospel three times.
Each time Bible opens to
the passion. Frances comes
out of cell and sees
Seraph - and received the
Stigmata. sealing Frances
with body of Suffering Christ.
St. Bonaventure - "After two days

and nights. Francis comes down as law giver with the prints of the Alter Christus. Francis immediately made a saint. There had not been major saints in Centuries.

SANCTUARIO
FRANCESCANO

La Montagna delle Stimmate.
Il Signore ti dia pace!
Philippians 2 - Though he was God ... 1182 Francis born into a time of both wealthmaking and stunning source of poverty. Monks of Subiaso gave portion Portuncula - of land - S M. deglia Angeli.

July 3. 2010 Climb Mount La Verna w/ Ed Berry and Artie Mastrolia -

with birds, show his imagination was an instrument that could work peace. His visit to the sultan of Egypt is a rare page of diplomacy with the Muslim world.

Francis was born into a time of great wealth-making that was also a stunning source of great poverty. Stigmatized with the wounds of the Christ, Francis became an alter-Christus, in the words of St Bonaventure 'after his days and nights [in prayer in La Verna] Francis came down as lawgiver'. The law of brotherly love he preached was synthesized in the della Robbia blue and white altarscreens, one of many defining artworks that in the Renaissance interpreted the legacy of Francis. It is summed up in an opposing nativity scene and a passion scene in often reproduced ceramic: a nativity with a passion beneath and a passion with a nativity beneath. Suffering and joy commingle. Poverty is acclaimed as a 'queen'. A version of the *Stabat Mater* is sung at Christmas. Francis came in a time when the dialogue between clerics and artists was constant and complementary. Isn't this the root of how the imagination serves peace? Simply put, putting nativity and the passion of Christ side-by-side is in essence saying 'I can see the baby in its mother's arms in the face of a suffering man', and 'I can see the suffering in potentia in the face of a baby'. Complaints against the vacuity of contemporary art have to be met with some upbraiding for our neglect of artists in recent times. Artists are struggling to articulate that tragic backdrop to our human condition because they have intuited through the tradition the comic vindication of the word made flesh. Artists too need to be upbraided for living off the flesh of the ecclesial salvation narrative without the critical accountability that would keep their voice toned and durable. Serrano's crucifixion in urine comes to mind, though I have always felt there is something elegiac about the image that is obscured by prankish context.

Altar Screen by Andrea della Robbia · focussed on Francis – 1223 – on Nativity crib · grecchio a hill town · Passion Scene inserted

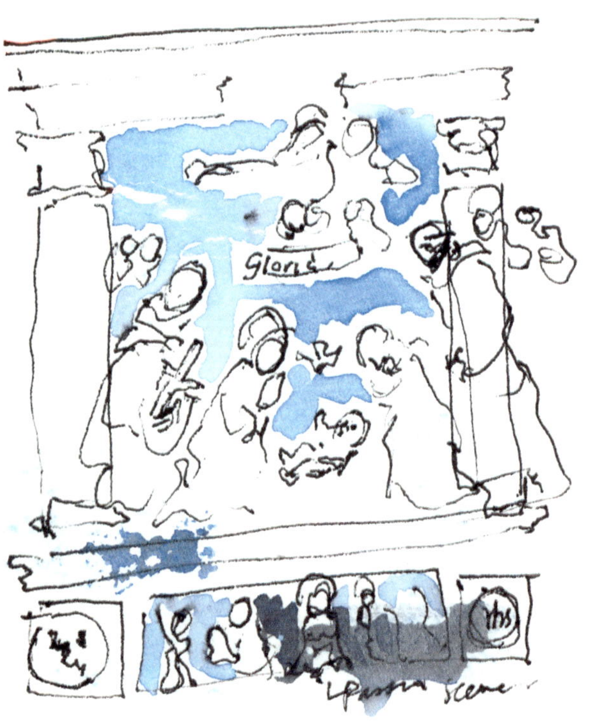

Madonna + Child Scene beneath passion Scene. Christmas version of Stabat Mater. Franciscan Spirituality

Early 15 c. art

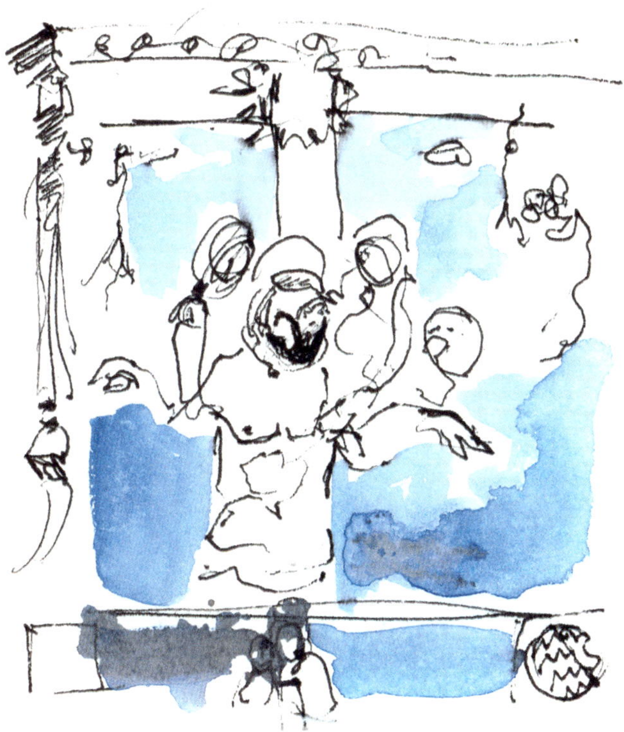

our Lady donating
girdle to St. Thomas.
subject of Altar
piece - DellaRobbia
are wks that looked
like marble. close
working of topic
of art by artists
and clergy - listening
to great homilies compares style
and content.
Early 1300's major pilgrimage
1548 year of bl. death. church begun

Arte de la lana – Flor.
woolguild paid the finishing
of church

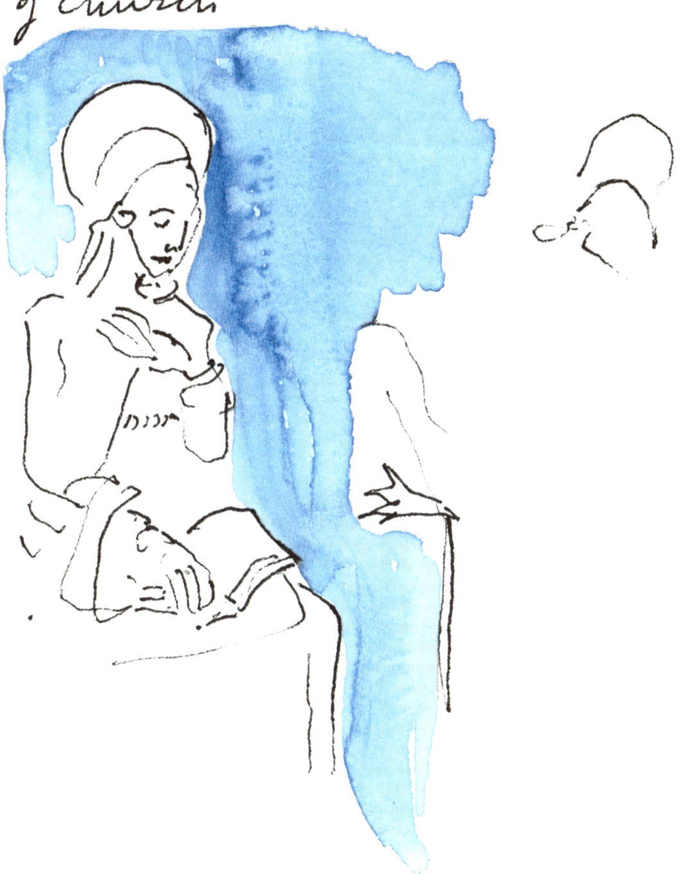

Following our ascetic morning with Francis is a waiting pullman for 16 of us who opted to visit the nearby birthplace of Michelangelo, Caprese di Michelangelo, for a meal at the restaurant of the nephew of a parishioner from Holy Trinity on the Upper West Side who spent years in service to Toscanini and to Vladimir and Wanda Horowitz. Mario Cheli's restaurant is appropriately named 'Il Rifugio'. He made seven variations on truffles and mushrooms that come nearby in earthy abundance. Creamy pools of cheese and cream flecked with truffles and bubbling in terracotta dishes followed a layered dome of mushrooms. A mossy brown growth of truffle formed a topsoil to hot beef. Concluding with soft, hot biscotti to dip in vin santo reinforces in taste and smell the path from humility to majesty that is a reward for an imagination steeped in the real and open to grace. We can make a god of food, but when food and art make necessity sublime it is an occasion for good conversation. Our conversation continued the theme: what can Italy teach us? The bus driver had a three o'clock job and had to get us back. Giuliana's sister Maria and her husband are Mario Chieli's mother and father. Giuliana is his aunt who lives in New York. It was important to Giuliana that I meet Maria and her husband, who thought there would be time to meet after the meal and sat at home patiently dressed, but there wasn't time and they followed the bus to Chiusi della

Verna. They stopped the bus at last in the middle of the street and they called for Don Andrea. She and her sister had almost starved during the war and still live with the effects. Their gentleness is animated by gratitude. I tell them that their son gave a gift to the Archdiocese of New York. Fr. Joe Fallon said it was like Babette's Feast. I don't think they saw the movie, but they understand without the explanation.

July 4th, Sunday. Siena

Fr. Sorgie celebrated the early mass singing. We have been celebrating a daily mass in the chapel at Pastor Angelicus. I like to hear the strong voices in response. Siena today. Another superstar saint to meet. St Catherine's head looks more like a glimpse at Edvard Munch's *The Scream.* I pray for my sister Kitty, whose patron saint is Catherine, and light a taper. Catherine was born in the neighborhood of San Domenico, the large plain barn of a Dominican church opposite the pink and green and white striated Duomo. A valley separates them filled with tumbling buildings. She was born in the year before the plague, 1347. My sister Molly said last summer that the plague proved the power of scholasticism, the fruit of the mendicant orders, because there is no other disaster to match the invisible horror of one in four Europeans dying so swiftly. Without a full soaking of philosophy the faith lives of Christians would never have been able to distinguish fate and suffering in the wake of that disaster.

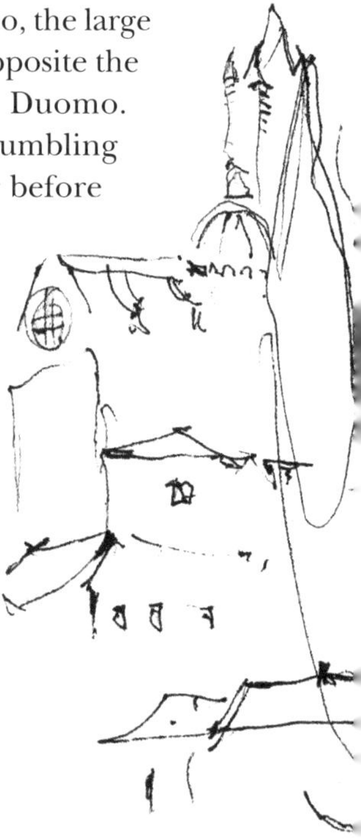

Catherine only lived 33 years. By the time most of us are just getting out of graduate schools with manicured opinions about how women needed the sexual revolution and reproductive rights to find liberation, this 20th of 22 children wrote and dictated books that were actually read. So much so, that her diplomacy in

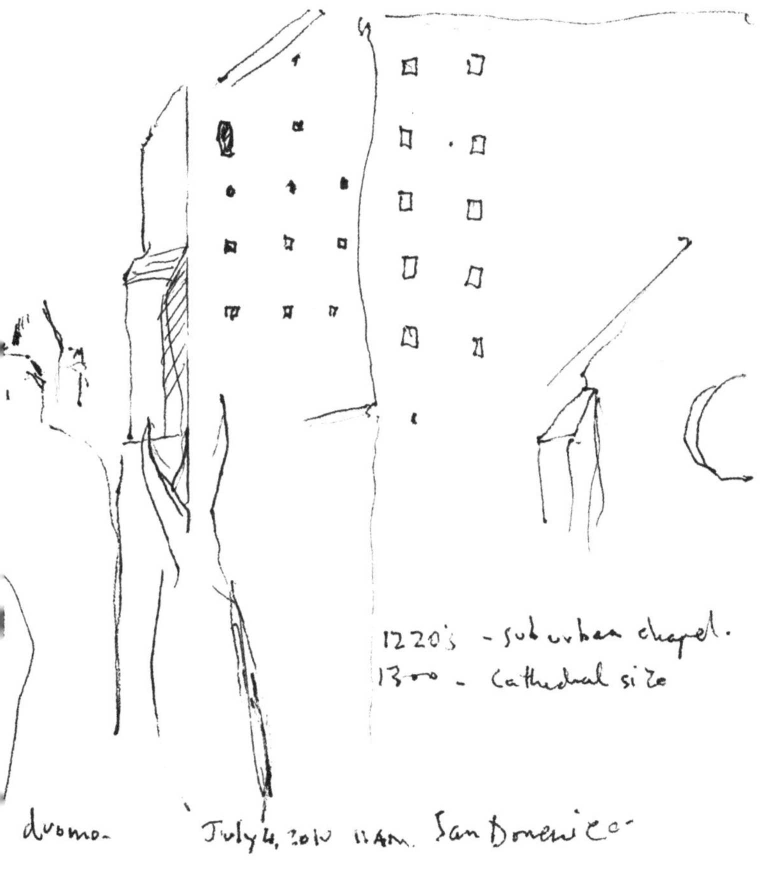

the Avignon court mediated the restoration of the papacy to Rome. Considering the backdrop of the divisions between the Holy Roman Emperor and the Pope that were condensed in the divisions between the Guelphs and the Ghibellines, her insights are clearly synthetic. Allen Tate, quoted in the first paragraph, features the story of St Catherine in the same essay. He maintains that her consolation of a murderer in the month before his execution in Siena is a seminal example of the symbolic imagination. She says that she will be there to receive his head. She is indeed there to catch the head and is splattered by the blood from the axe. She says that she could smell the blood of the lamb. Tate, a convert to Catholicism and a proponent of understatement, cites the example because, he claims, she clearly never loses sight of the literal blood and the victim. The symbolic imagination can bridge the gap between the literal and the signified. In the back of the church she found a private place to pray before the eucharist. She exchanged her heart with Jesus and received the stigmata.

Another figure closely associated with Siena is Bernardine. In front of the church a large piazza was often filled with thousands. Strategically placed big-voiced assistants listened and repeated his slow speech, in case you wanted to know how such a large crowd could hear one man without amplification. Apparently, it worked better. Bernardine knew his audience and lifted the sunburst with the 'IHS' in the middle at strategic moments

St Cath. 1347. born year before plague 1380 died 33yrs - family house near to house. prayed often.

1221 MARY IN MAJESTY. GUIDO of SIENA

Italian Byzantine. "Odiggiatra" mary indicates Jesus is the way.

- prayer before eucharist.
- received hidden Stigmata
- exchanged hearts.

late medieval mysticism

St. Catherine Head. 1550 Sotovin. Sienese artist wked w/ Rafael.

DUCCIO DE BUONISEGNA.
SIMONE DE MARTINI

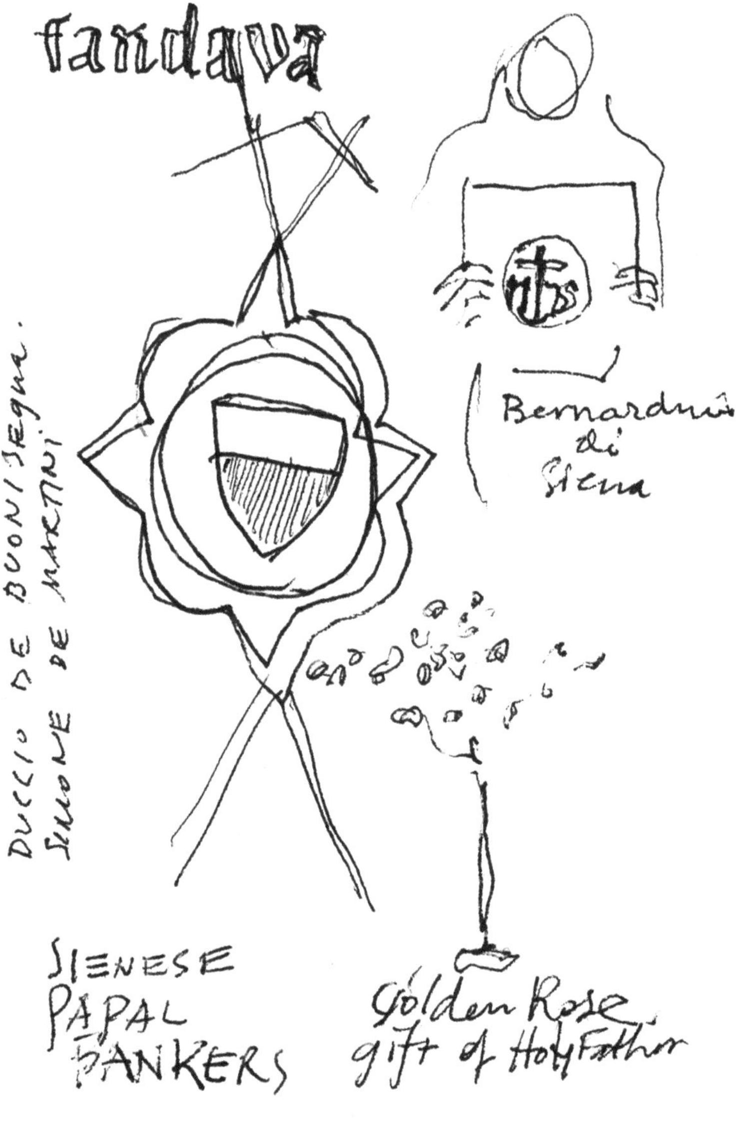

tandava

Bernardino di Siena

DUCCIO DE BUONINSEGNA
SIMONE DE MARTINI

SIENESE
PAPAL
BANKERS

Golden Rose
gift of Holy Father

when he suspected he might lose their attention. Professor Verdon says 'IHS' was a variation on the name Jesus. James Joyce says it means 'I have suffered.' That is true too.

We visit St Catherine's home, the kitchen church. The lapis blue walls and the gold stars are foil for jewel-like paint on wooden-panel portraits of nobles and saints that punctuate the space. Catherine's kitchen pot hangs off the wall below the altar on a hook as if never moved.

It has been two days since the Palio, a bareback horse race in the shell-shaped Campo in the heart of Siena. Flags of the winning *contrada,* one of 17 neighborhoods of Siena, dominate the square. 'Selva' has oak leaves on its flag. A portion of the earth covering the stone stretches in front of the Town Hall. Romulus' brother Remus was more evidently not killed, as the Romans claim, but made it up here to found the city. Everywhere are statues of mother wolf and the fabled fat babies suckling her. We enter the town hall and climb up to a large upper room which pays homage to the union of Sienese bankers to the Papacy. A golden rose, a gift of the Holy Father, grows like a miraculous bonsai on a shelf.

Monsignor Verdon draws us into the parliament chamber to point out a fresco on good government. Happy fields, a lady on horseback is fashionably plump at the pink gates of the city, scaffolding on a tower and balanced workmen is a clue to how Brunelleschi built the Duomo in Florence without scaffolding. In the eternally blue sky a feminine figure of wisdom floats over the throne and other virtues stand in attendance. On the opposite wall bad government is ruled by *superbia,* pride. A delicate neck of a girl is crushed under a golden yoke. Other vices engulf the stormy scene. The city and country crumble in misery in the distance. A good morality tale for Independence Day.

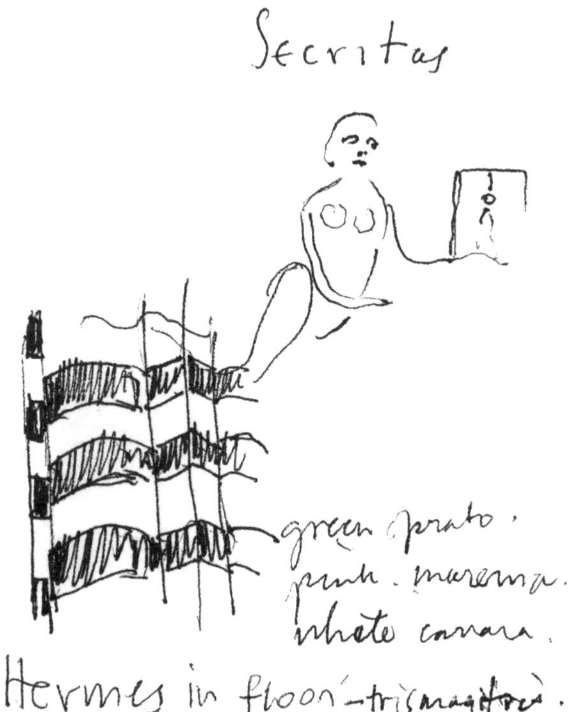

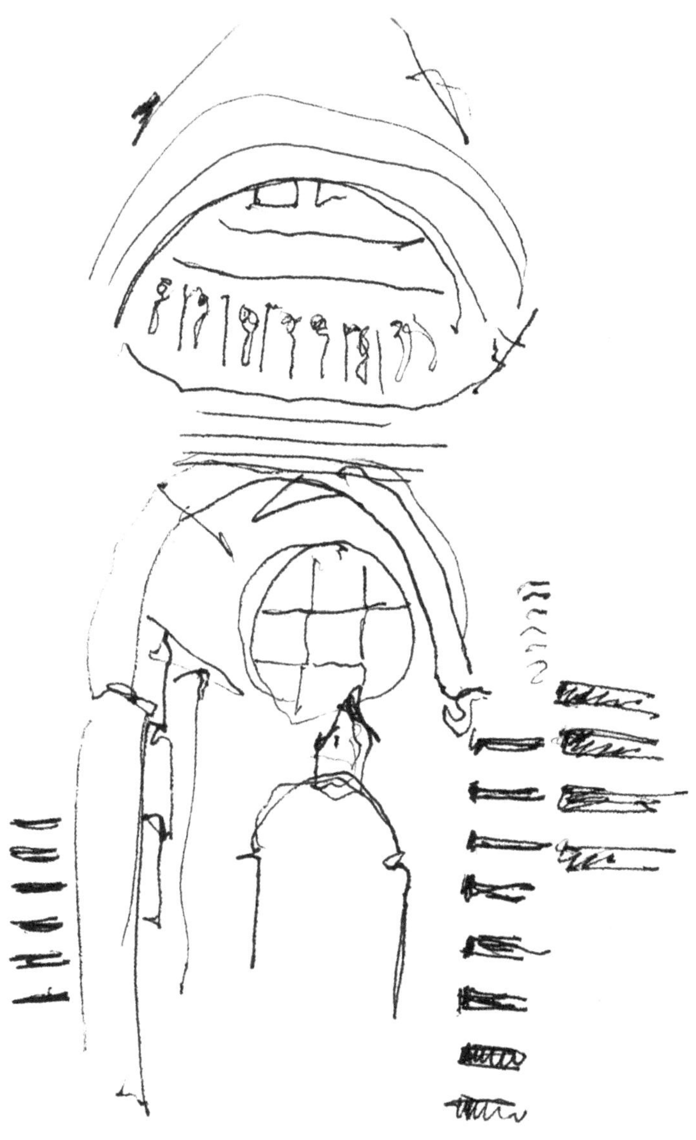

After lunch we meet over by the Duomo. The first person to greet you in the floor in front of the main doors is Hermes Trismegistus, a pagan philosopher. The Duomo is populated by loads of unbaptized pagans, though baptized by desire. The library sports a classical fountain of three nudes. Why not? Pinturicchio tells that proud tale of a shamelessly successful Sienese cleric who becomes Pope. Elevated to one side of the sanctuary the ambo roils in little bodies. The whole piece is in marble and the figure of the resurrected Christ is so real, leaning out, he is about to speak. This early realism is an exceptional piece and the object of emulation. An inspiration in particular to the Sienese artist Duccio, whose Madonna was the Metropolitan Museum of Art's most recent and most expensive purchase. We conclude with a visit to the treasury and too short a time before Duccio's windows. We have a moment for a *gelato*. Some secure the prized *pan forte* before we mount the bus again. Dario our driver gets us back just in time for dinner. The temperature drops from 33 degrees Celsius to 22 (91 to 73 degrees Farenheit). I fetch a bowl of ice for spirits to celebrate independence after dinner.

July 5th, Monday. Florence

We start early to Florence but it still takes a long time. We are a block from the Duomo and Monsignor Verdon meets us. We enter a side door. Fr. Sorgie shares a Sienese joke on how the Duomo in Florence is like Florence itself, all flourish on the outside and nothing on the inside. Monsignor doesn't like the joke but laughs politely anyway. He whisks us into the *feriale* sacristy with ceilings as high as a planetarium. An old priest at the desk brightens and said that he was in Poughkeepsie in 1966. Fr. Alexander Pacchia. The sacristan has albs and stoles for everyone. He adjusts Fr. Tom Kelly's. When the bell rings and we process the tourists hush for a moment and then resume. Monsignor Tim Verdon preaches. He has enjoyed the opportunity to present the context of the art to fellow American priests. Artie Mastrolia will run off to get a gift for him – a pen from a Florentine 'scriptorium'.

After mass a tour of the bishop's sacristy. The lavabo is an angel urinating into a marble sink. The *gardinarium* in the rear is a wooden door that uncovers a set of stairs down to a plot of earth for a toilet. Vestments are under the center vesting table whose bottom is lower than the floor to accommodate the length of the garments. Other advantages to the sacristy? Bronze doors help ward

July 5, 2010 Sacristy.
Concelebrating mass
at Duomo.
Alexander Pacchio - Rev.
Spent time in 1968 in Poughkeep.

Mass over around 12:15
At Marian chapel.

Sacristy
feriale
—
Sacristea
de la
Messe.
is decorated
in marquetry
panels.
'fully
illusionistic
panels
invented by Felipo Brunelleschi
"why artists can't make lines obey
the logic.

all precii
woods expd
in apparent

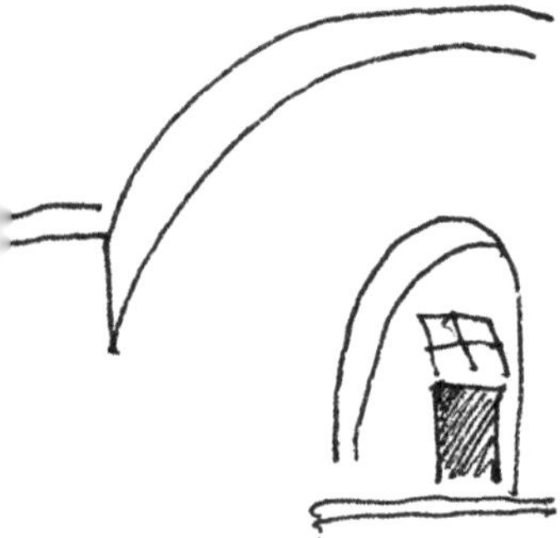

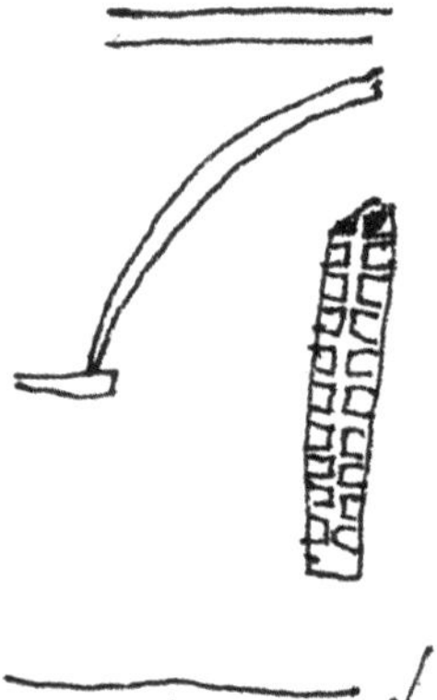

giardinum-
fresh earth toilet

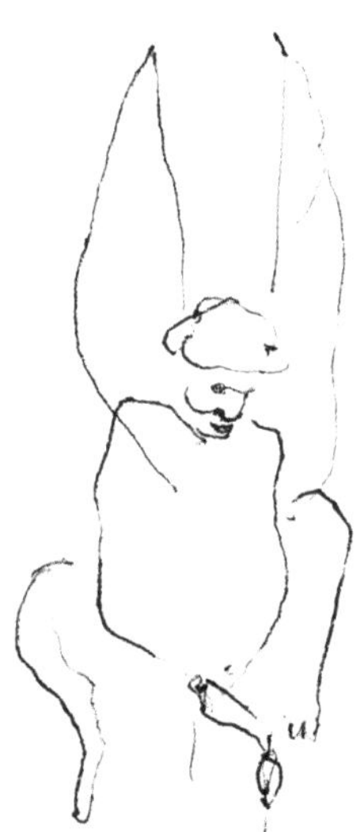

lavabo is an angel urinating
vesture sunk under table

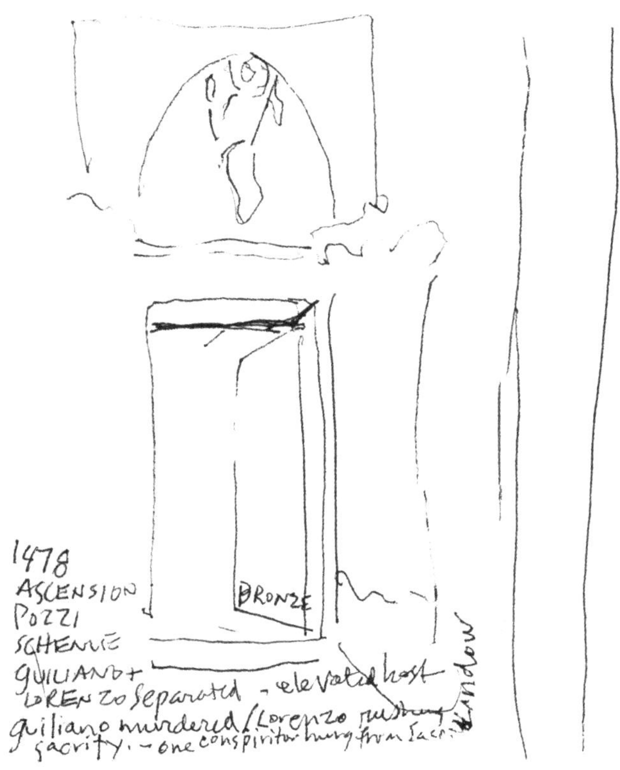

off assassins. In 1478, on Ascension Thursday, the Pazzi family schemed to assassinate Giuliano and Lorenzo Medici during mass at the elevation of the host when their guards were distracted. Lorenzo's guards caught the plot in time and rushed him into the sacristy, closing the doors until reinforcements arrived. One of the perpetrators was hung out the window of the sacristy.

1439. COUNCIL OF FLO
RENCE COSIMO THE
ELDER. BROUGHT C. TO
FL. healing rift betw
East + Western Church
three yrs. BZ. Joh + Eug. IV
under open dome 1453
OTTOMAN TURK. EAST wants help

In 1439 Florence hosted the wandering Council of Florence at the invitation of Cosimo the Elder. The Emperor in Byzantium saw the proverbial Arabic on the doorstep and was eager for a truce with the West in hopes of military aid against the Ottoman Turks. Bishops John and Eugenio IV were dispatched to Florence with other bishops from the East. The Florentine Church embraced learning Greek with alacrity and the Fathers expressed their hospitality to the Eastern Church by setting up a Greek school for the Latin bishops. It only underscored Western openness to learning and Eastern intransigence. Disappointingly, with all that effort, as soon as the truce was declared the treaty was renounced. Armenia and the Lebanese churches aligned with Rome, however. POSTLONGASDISPUTATIONES *after long discussions…* Is written on the tablet by the sacristy.

Armenians accepted - union w/ Rome. Set up greek School for Latin Bishops and helped enter into Patristic mindset.

POSTLONGASDISPUTATIONES

After long discussions.

1420 Brunelleschi finished 1434

Eugenius + entourage came from Sm Novella to Duomo on raised platform.

Dome 43 m in diameter. (same as Pantheon.) competition to cover opening.

60m to opening — Brun. built w/out scaffolding. floating wk platform.

Rising above us is the famous dome that must have impressed the participants of the council. The octagonal base is 43 meters wide, the same as the Pantheon and 60 meters to the opening. Higher than Hagia Sophia. How to complete the dome was open to an international competition, the happy custom of Florence that won so much acclaim. The hometown boy – Filippo Brunelleschi – was given no special consideration. He was an effective campaigner with a tantalizing way of teasing intrigue out of the process. His claim: he can build the dome without scaffolding. He wins without divulging the plain secret. He created open scaffolding from the masonry ports with timber and vaulted upwards row by row.

In twenty years another spectacle of politics and collusion with church and state. This time the *David* of Michelangelo began as a series of prophets for the interior of the Duomo, but following Medici's expulsion the City Council commissioned the statue for itself. Michelangelo re-conceived the work as a model of a civic hero, slightly frowning over the work of statecraft. He won a space for it before the prominent town hall. I am drawing furiously and scribbling notes. Then there is a painting of my hero Dante off to the side. We are discussing the visuals of the renaissance and not the literature. You can't do it all, but who else embodies an appeal to classical direction than the poet whose hero Virgil appeared at the moment of

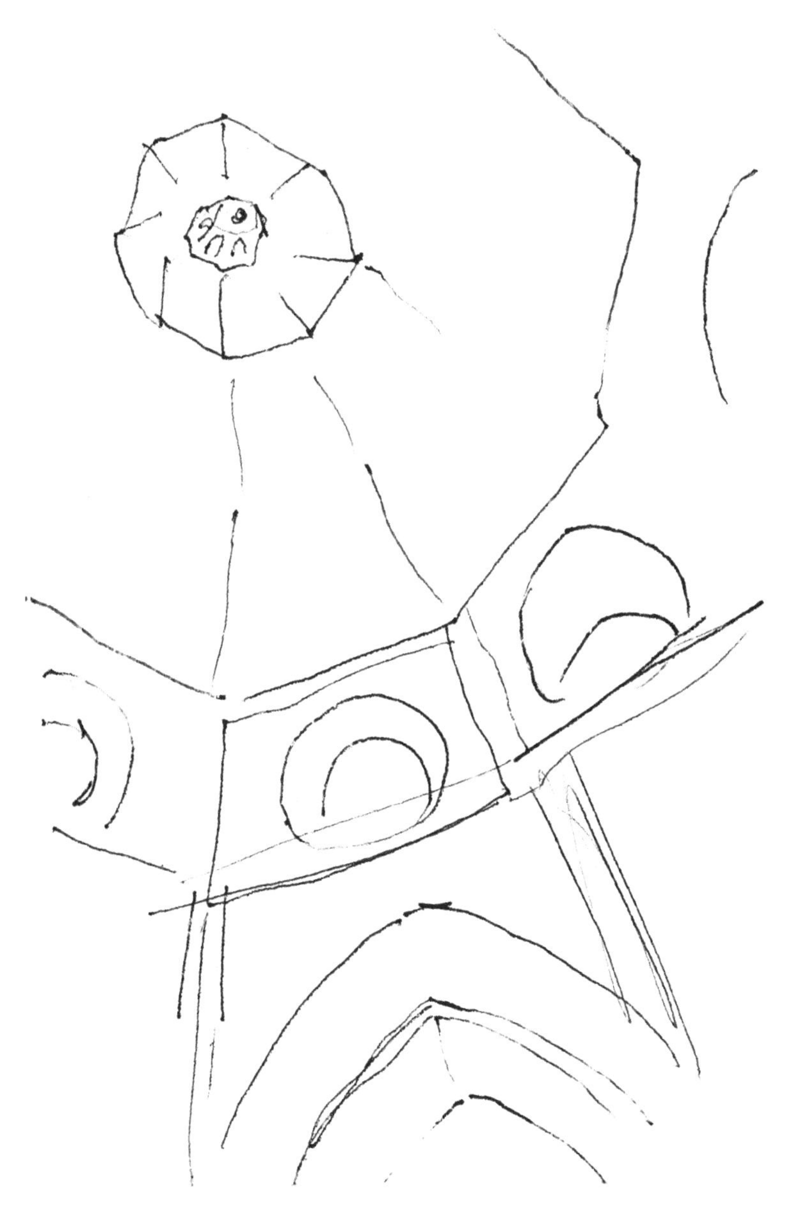

DAVID of MICHELANGELO
1501 – 1504 – for Duomo –
meanwhile Medici thrown out.
Changed plans and placed in
civic context in Town Hall –
not in religious context
Bp Guisseppe – Vitori
Dome finished 1436.

PAINTING OF DANTE

his desperation. I had a homily prepared for Dante in the morning which will be delivered tomorrow.

Joe Fallon and I break for lunch together as the others break off to forage. There is so much to see in Florence I wonder why we can't stay on and catch dinner on the road back. The proposal sounds good at lunch but loses steam. 'You can always come back'. Yes that is true. Don't do too much.

We convene at the Baptistry, an entirely separate building in front of the Duomo. I remember a guide singing a note that was completed into a full chord, not by a harmonizing choir, but by the eight sides of the architecture. The eighth day signifies that day which will not end. Our attention turns to the dome, built over, as it happens, living water. Originally a temple of Mars. The god Mars, by the way, always bullies his way into prime real estate. The Romans that repelled the foul king Tarquin decided not to divide the spoil of the king's wheat that grew in the Campus Martius in Rome. Rather they dumped it in the Tiber and it miraculously grew into the Isola Tiberina. (Great hospital there. You can drink at the bar as you convalesce). Columns from the old temple are reused. The feet of Christ grip the disk at the world's edge. They are large and prominent, forcing perspective ever upward. He is 8 meters tall seated (about 26 feet). The just and the damned are separated, the souls of the just leaping out. Can't wait. The damn

1000 – 1100's Baptistry

temple of Mars –
Columns from Roman Temp

8m is tall. seated.

Souls of JUST

DAMNED

child.

Early ✝ Commun. in Flo.
Chose this fountain source
from old Roman walls - inspired
by Ambrose in Milan -
8 DAYS.
OCtave

can't be moved, must be pried out. The devils have special tools and talons for the work. Among the just a child is running at play. It is the type of small detail that makes the whole scene come alive, somewhat like the way the handprints of Picasso's daughter at the base of *Guernica* set off the newsprint lines above it. There is the mouth of Satan as Dante saw it, munching on a sinner.

Embers of the Easter fire, started by flint stolen fair and square from the Holy Sepulcher in Jerusalem, restarts the homefires of Florentines. That would be a worthwhile ritual to adopt in the United States after an Easter mass, except we don't have homefires anymore. A better ritual in Florence on Easter is the team of white oxen with gilded horns that pull a box on wheels in front of the Duomo before the Easter Sunday mass. Flags somersault through the air. During the Gloria of the mass the doors open wide and a fuse hanging from the tail of a mechanical bird is lit. A roman candle in its belly propels the bird suspended from a wire down the center of the nave. It strikes the box and sets off fireworks. The bird returns at highspeed to hit a post over the high altar and drop harmlessly on a pillow until next year. The fireworks send in smoke and light into the rear of the church. Monsignor Timothy Verdon says that the most dour cleric, muttering 'I can't believe we do this' is won over by the spectacle. I don't know how we could get oxen and a fireworks box up Fifth Avenue, but perhaps something could be worked out.

IOHA̅NES ORICELLARIVS PAV·
F AN S AL·MCCCCCLXX

ALBERTI INVENTED
THE SCROLLS
To Bridge
Medieval &
Renaissance.

S.M. de NOVELLA

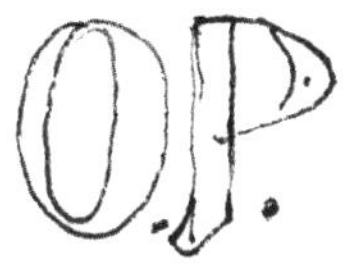

EMBERS restart homefires.
17C florentines came to church

SMNOVELL 1179 gothic
1240 - trancept
1st Gothic in Italy
Cistercian Gothic

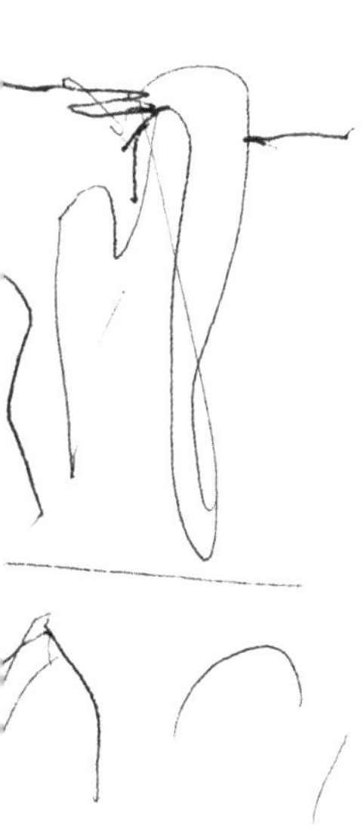

great rose window back of church

altar front of church

wall

originally farm behind church.

Giotto - christo patzien

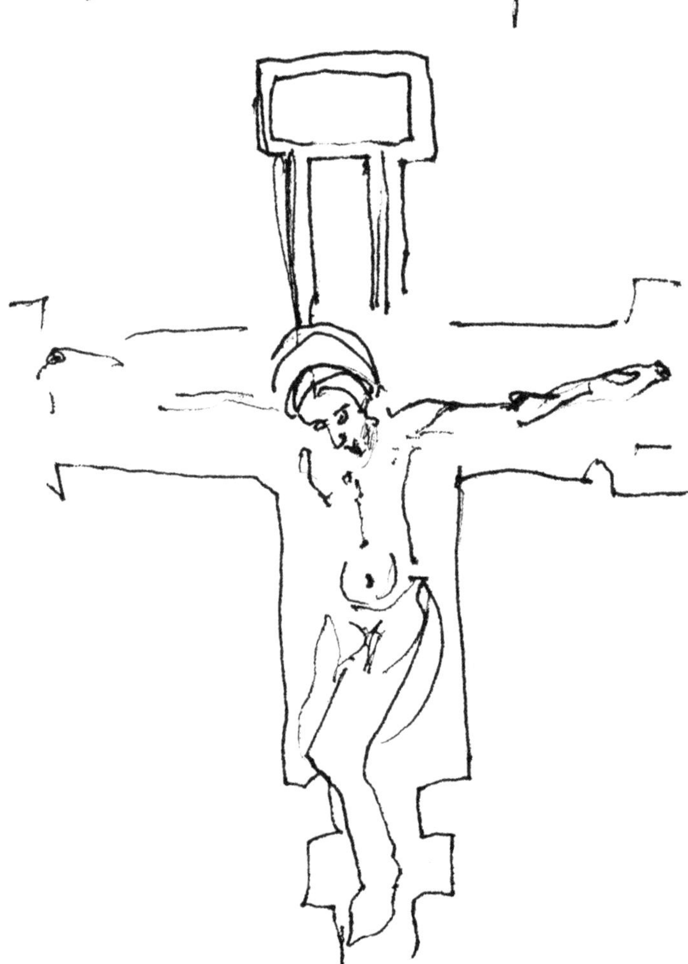

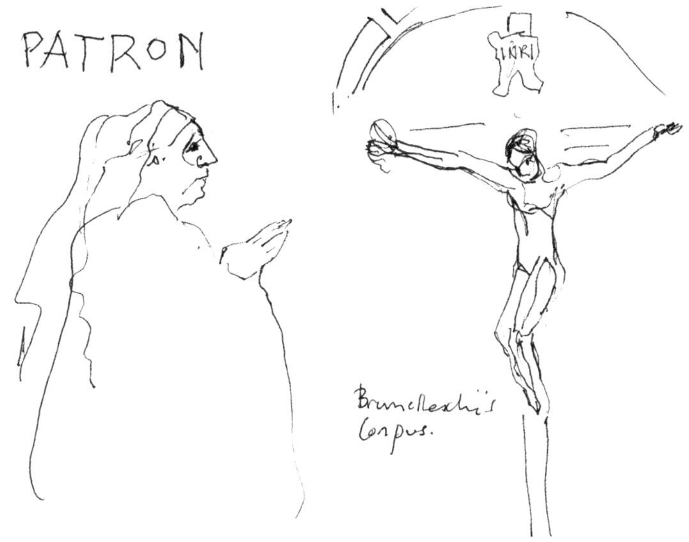

We walk briskly to Santa Maria Novella, the only Dominican church of its era with a fancy façade. Great art means having to walk past the Giotto crucifix because you need to dwell on Masaccio. 'Big hulking Tommasaccio', as he was called. He sought advice from Brunelleschi. They tacked in nails in the stucco and hung strings to devise the schema for perspective to greet pilgrims at the door. The Virgin Mary is a woman in widow's weeds pointing her hand towards the cross, gazing outwards. A skeleton beneath the painting bears the inscription below: 'I was as you are, and I am as you will be', a memento mori, but with a twist since the crucifixion is the center of our attention and the center of perspective. The patrons are flanking the scene. The corpus is Brunelleschi's.

Big hulking Tom Massachio.

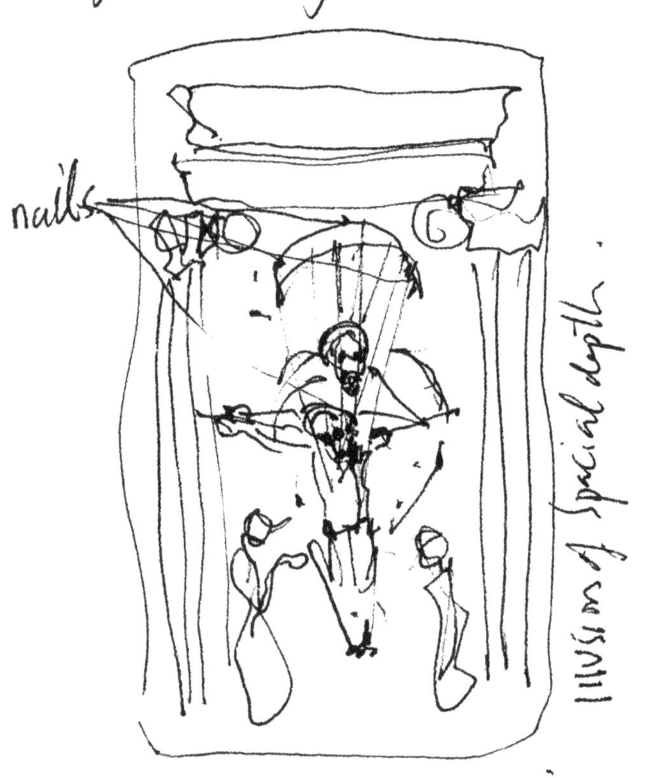

Massachio + Brunelleschi.

pillasters.
perspective constrn.

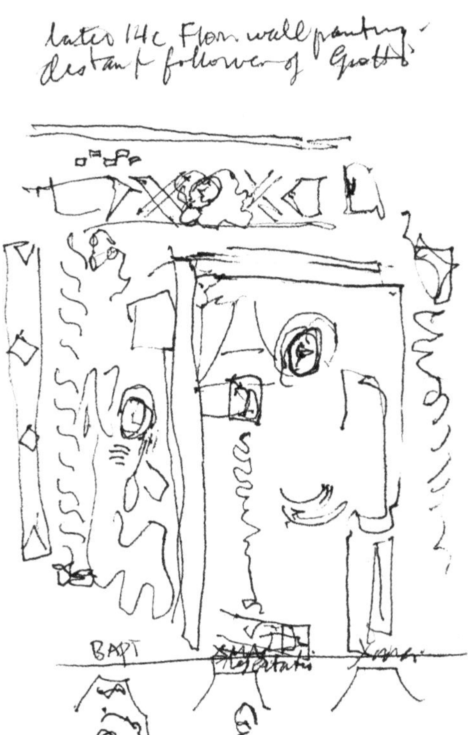

We stop at an Annunciation towards the rear of the church. 'The virgin's bed is neatly made' comments Monsignor Verdon. The realism requires attention to details to control the scene. It is refreshing to reach Ghirlandaio's *Visitation*, the familiar rear end of the figure leaning over the wall to look down in the valley, a technique to mask a problem with landscape perspective.

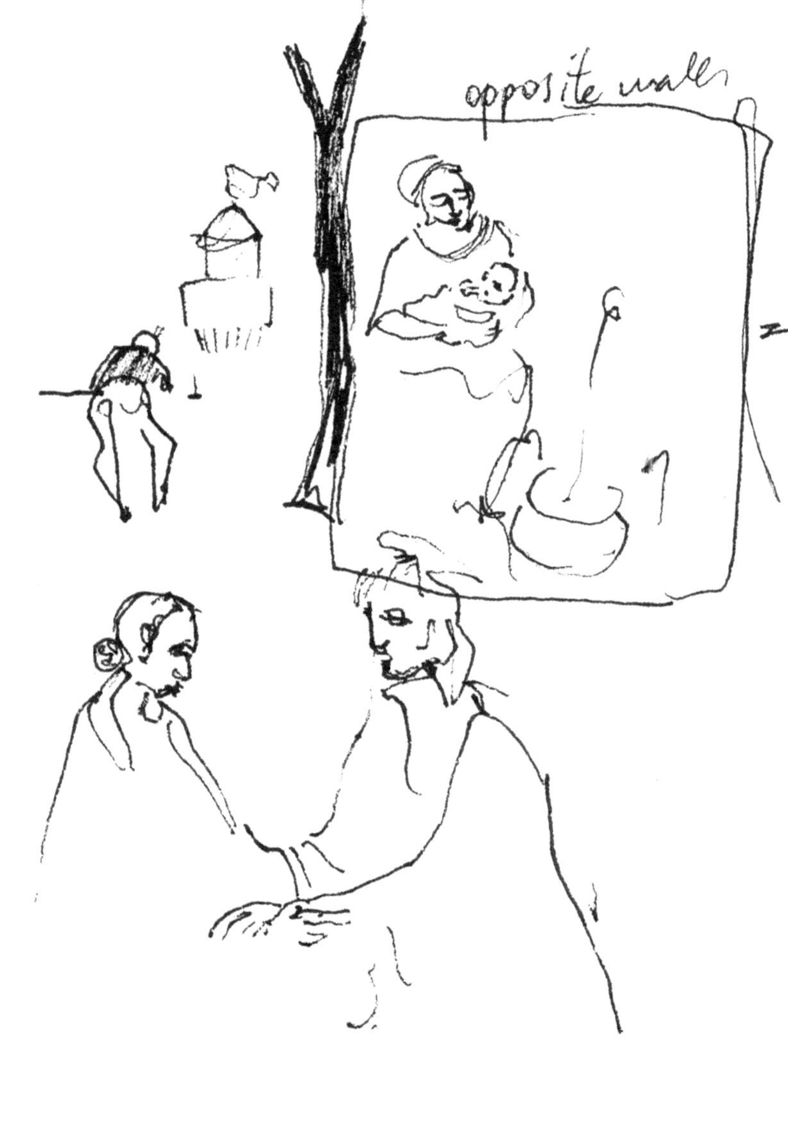
opposite walls

Domenico Ghirlandajo 1490.

I run to the Farmacia Santa Maria Novella around the corner to get a bottle of Sicilian water and make it back to the bus in time for *gelato*. We bid farewell to Fr. Sorgie and Fr. Bisognano, who are heading onto Rome. The mountain road is familiar now. Dinner and the world cup. It is good after all to decompress and reflect.

Sansepolcro 6 july 2010

mass in morning. a miniature renaissance Florence –

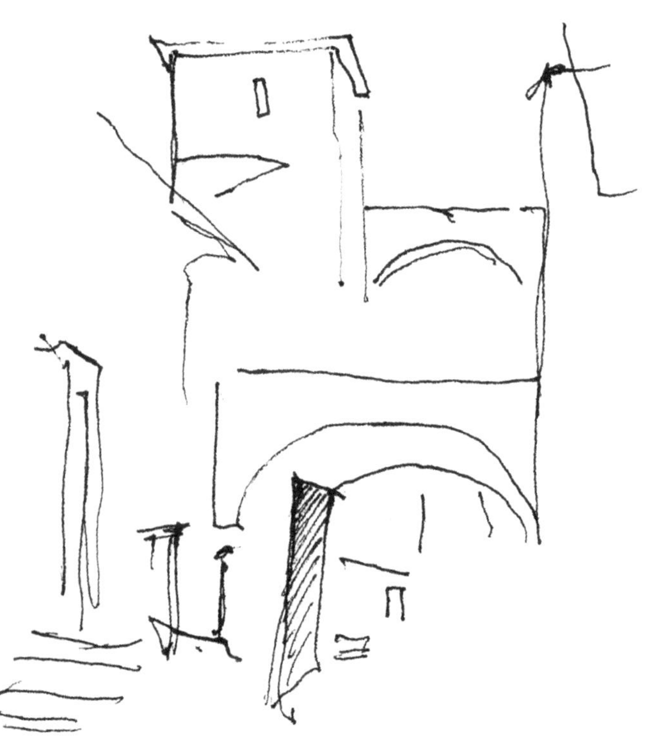

July 6th, Tuesday. Sansepolcro

My turn for mass. I include in the homily the four levels of interpretation mentioned in Dante's letter to Cangrande following the publication of the *Divine Comedy*. Cangrande was having some difficulty grasping the poem and wanted some help. To the lay person interested in cultivating the symbolic imagination, these four levels at the very least help hone a critical eye on what makes a great painting, or a great poem. Dante states that the pilgrim in his *Comedy* is on a literal pilgrimage, therefore the first level is the literal level. The loss of the literal can make or break art. The second level is the allegorical level. Simply put, an image can stand for something else: a pilgrim can allegorically be everyman. Thirdly, there is the anagogical level of interpretation, how there is a mystical or heavenly interpretation. To Dante this really was a political level of interpretation. How we form the mystical body is the focus of this level on interpretation. Dante is concerned with the life of the city, and in particular his beloved Florence. His work is a map of the political divisions and essential tensions that inhabit every city and those peculiar to Florence. Finally, there is a analogical level of interpretation. Coleridge described what it meant to interpret art at this level was as a fragmentary 'participation in the reality that is signified.' Fortified with Dante, the eucharist, itself the perfect 'analogy', and *caffelatte* we greet our gentle bus driver, Dario.

Holy
FACE VOLTO SANTO
dates to 8-9c time of Charlemagne – carved by Nicodemus –

King who reigns from cross

one trunk of wood

Annunciu Fortunarius contemp source

cross as Throne

Monumental Christ – rare.

A short distance from Chiusi della Verna is Sansepolcro. The town is a miniature Renaissance Florence, with grand three-tiered palazzi. It was here that the promising Piero della Francesca chose to live in a sleepy provincial reserve rather than pursue the fame of Florence. In the church is the *Volto Santo,* the holy face, a crucifix whose corpus is a single piece of wood and dating to the time of Charlemagne in the 8th and 9th centuries. The image is attributed to Nicodemus, Jesus' night visitor, and has a calm tilted head, a slightly forked beard and long hair flowing into subtle twists. He is enthroned on the cross wearing the chasuble and stole of a priest. The piece is well lit and the features do have a soulful aliveness to them. His monumental form is rare and compellingly sympathetic. We all love this piece for its tenderness. In a nearby fresco, a bishop with a gash down his pate turns out to be Thomas a Becket. Rome is saying you mustn't kill bishops at mass. You must not kill bishops at anytime, but especially not at mass. For that matter avoid assassinations at mass too. Thomas is holding the knife that killed him and gazing at it intently.

Around the corner is the Borgo museum. Monsignor Verdon walks us past a painting and then stops. 'Now this would be useful to look at'. It is not a great painting but it is commissioned by the local guilds and so it was with Piero della Francesca; whose paintings were also commissioned by the local guilds. Only look what he did with the little he was given. As you turn the corner the vision has the effect of the long-awaited sun. This is the painting of the virgin whose open cape protectively enfolds the guild members, all knee high. Her eyes are inwardly drawn, tender and reflective. Her hair is oddly shaved so that she is almost bald, as was the fashion of the day. The background is all gold, like Klimt would do. Monsignor Verdon says that Piero may have more in common with modern abstract painting. I can see where he is at home in the medium and loves the sanctuary of open space. No rush to fill in every thing.

If that were not enough of a thrill, the Resurrection in the next room is inescapably profound. Christ is stepping out of the grave with his left leg up on the ledge. Here is art working with the difficult balance between human and divine. Behind him, the Victor Rex, are trees to his right in winter, leafless and brittle, to the left full with fresh leaves. The heads of the soldiers rest on the sepulcher their eyelids poised to open.

Piero della Francesca
chose to live in this local

MIA | contraternity of mercy.

Inward looking eyes.
highly intellectual
Sedes Sapientiae

1445
1454/60

victor rex

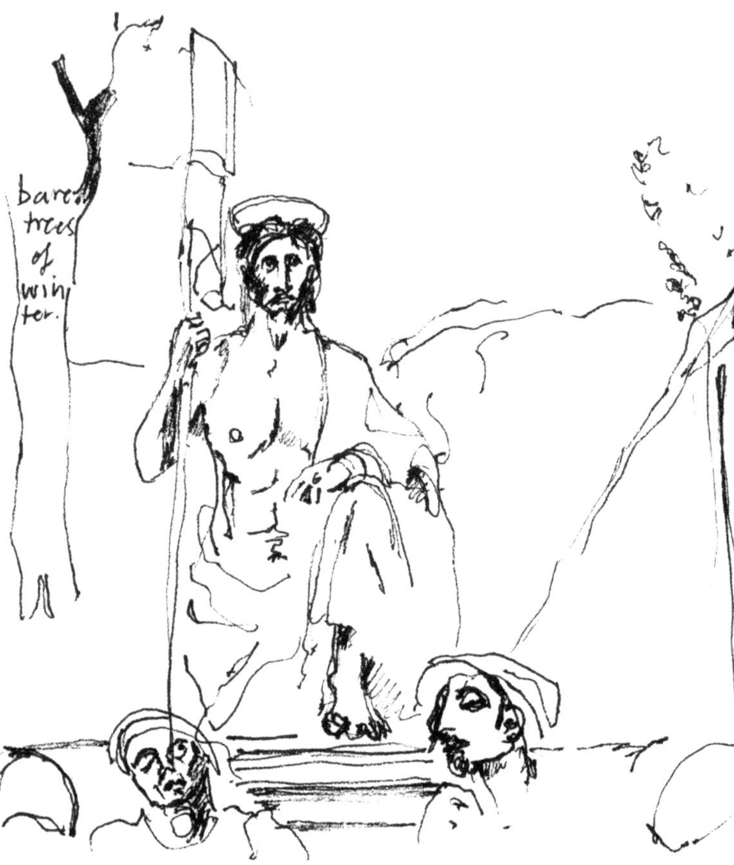

Monsignor Verdon closed with a reflection on Vatican II. Fifty or a hundred years is easily needed to interpret such a formidable Council, he said. It seems that it has hardly begun. The confidence that we should have that the Good News is a universal Good News should compel us to cultivate a symbolic imagination that is part of the living dialogue that shares what percolates up through the human imagination. That seems to appropriately reflect the spirit of Vatican II. Just as civilization can rise and fall, so too the life of faith in Christian community can suffer demise or be revitalized. The relationship between the Church and artists should be respectfully two-way.

It is interesting that our American presupposition that the radical separation of Church and State is the best of all possible worlds was subtly challenged on this purview of late medieval and renaissance art. The Church seemed to hold the State in check and vice versa. Sometimes the State wanted to own the Church. Many times the opposite was true too. Boundaries between the sacred and the profane require constant alignment and realignment, which is part of the ineluctable tension in human life.

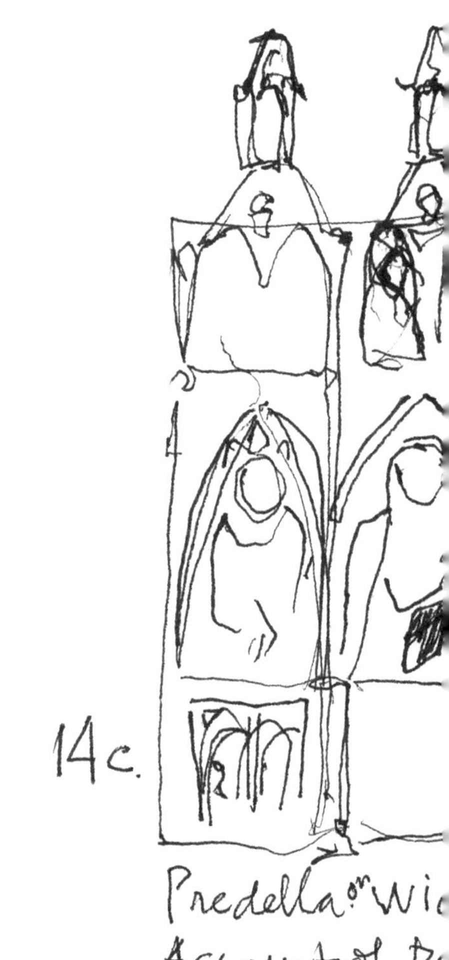
14c.
Predella on
Account of

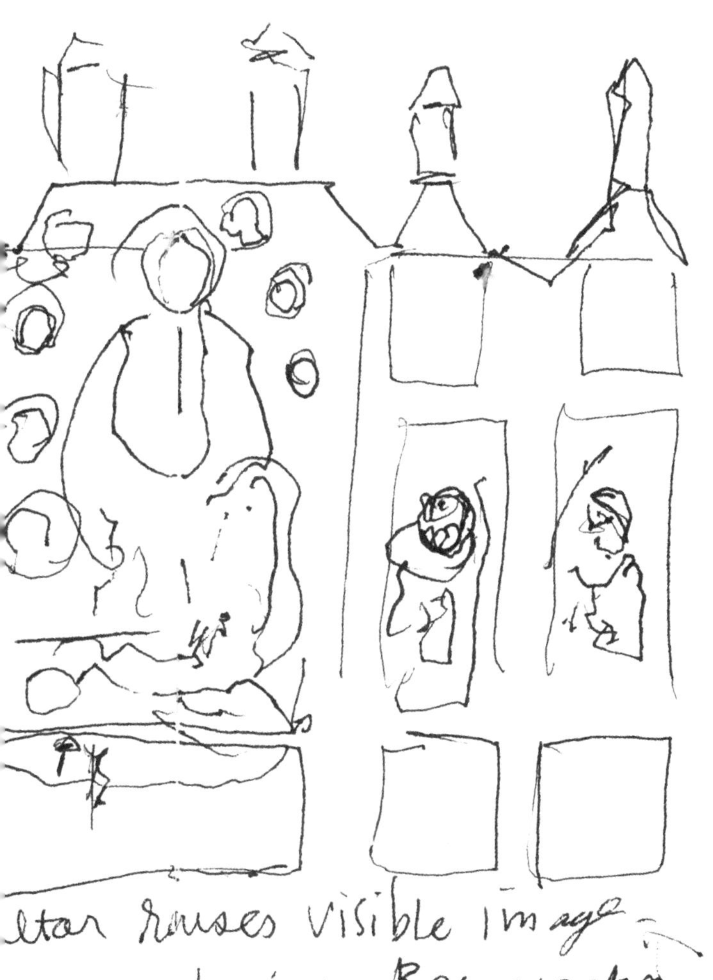

ltar rouses visible image

on emphasis on Resurrection

In the evening we assembled again. Monsignor Verdon had returned to Florence. We have an *amaro* to share and we discuss our impressions of the art we saw and our relation to art in the Church as such. Many expressed an openness to art in their parishes and cited examples of how that had been implemented, from commissioning original art to recognizing the existing art in the parish. Commonly, there was a distaste for modern or contemporary art. As an artist and a priest I can appreciate the current gulf between artists and priests. The two camps are deeply suspicious of each other for similar reasons. Since I have long collaborated with artists, I can offer a some pointers to priests and lay people alike:

Just start doing art. We need to see that great art was not just the product of genius. A great deal of anonymous and unimportant art was the foundation that made great art possible. Art inhabits the practical world. It is there ready to tackle spatial and temporal problems. This is where new forms emerge.

Art is not permanent. Good workmanship can make it long-lived, but even if long-lived it can be moved and changed, improved. It can be destroyed too, for better or for worse.

Art does not have to cost a lot of money. Materials can be very simple. Time, space, light, a living and understanding community can compensate a lot for an artist. Some churches have the above in abundance and some even have money. Usually those with money also have committees. Better to have a Medici who had as much vision as he had cash.

No decorators allowed. You can tell a real artist because they hate it when art is treated as a subset of interior decorating. Priests should understand this especially when we are treated as decoration at the wedding.

Manage your expectations. You may want the *Pietá* for your parish. Wouldn't that be nice? If you haven't noticed from the tour of Tuscany, it is hard to do new and exciting art in Italy because it is hard to compete with the old art. Unfortunately, Italy is a bit of a museum. New art, however, can be done in New York. New art in fact is done in New York. New York is the center of the art world and it is odd that the Church here has no real relationship with the prominent artists here in the City. The Church offers artists something very valuable: a transcendent narrative as well as potentially meaningful space for art. In the movies why is the backdrop of a church scene invariably a Catholic church?

Church, State and Art want to get to know each other. We have the wherewithal to generate great art in the New York Church. Just put the right ingredients together. For instance, it is the centennial of Catholic Charities this year. The spiritual father of Catholic Charities is Pierre Toussaint, a Haitian barber who hailed from our original cathedral. Since St Patrick's Old Cathedral was raised to the status of a basilica last year, uniting the celebration of Catholic Charities' milestone and elevating the sacred space within the basilica would be in order. I suggest a sacred floor be commissioned that would be on par with the floors in its brethren in Europe. It should be in wood, which is more appropriate to us in the United States. I was inspired by the wooded floor in the chapter room at the Camaldoli's Monastery. Given Cardinal O'Connor's particular love of that monastery that could be an inspirational context for the design. The design of a sacred floor could be granted to a prominent designer here in New York. Marc Newson would be interesting. University students in Ljubljana, Slovenia specializing in woodcraft, Slovenians are some of Europe's most esteemed woodworkers. Students who desire to follow in the same tradition could be given residency in the Slovenian national church on St Mark's Place and the wood could be harvested, milled and air-cured on the Homelands Foundation estate in Amenia, NY. Funding for the wood at least would be a part of their operational expenses. The students would require a stipend. Remaining funding is likely to be abundant for a work of this prominence. Just a thought.

July 7th, Wednesday. Venice

Seven hours to drive to Venice. John Ruvo said, after crossing the Po, that he thought it would have been wider. I don't know if he thinks less of Caesar as a result. Our guide greets us when we arrive in Venice and we lose Ed Barry right away. In the coming hours we all get lost in some way into this mysterious city. 'Venice is a delicate and miraculous old lady that requires much attention' says our guide, Gabriele di Moro. Old Romans and Phoenicians fled the boatless Barbarians swarming on the shore into the safety of the lagoon and sunk timber into the mud which happily turned to stone. 200 separate islands were united over the years with the diplomacy of bridges. Each island had their own church until Napoleon tore down 70 of them. After more than 1500 years the islands did not disintegrate, but Venice is sinking. A lock system is being built in the lagoon to keep the sea at bay. Our boat plows into the famous sea of color that the marble and water refract. Canals of this sort could be a solution to New Orleans. To the right is the pasta factory that Frank Sinatra thought would make a great casino. His friends at Hilton bought it eventually and made it into a hotel. The story goes that the owners were not going to sell it to him. How did Frank always get his way?

Fondamenta Zattere is the name of our boat stop, Grand Central in the discreet size of a kiosk. A *gelato* counter in the wall opposite the church dispenses emergency relief to the heat. Good luck learning Italian: the word for fork – *forchetta* – is 'spirón' in the Venetian dialect. Half an hour brisk walking will take you to the opposite side of Venice. After stowing away our bags at the Don Orione, we were passing each other in alleys and around corners as if each meeting is an odd coincidence. Santa Maria della Salute on the tip of the island is the first stop to take in in one view as much of Venice as I can.

July 8th, Thursday. Venice

This is the last day of an organized tour. We head to San Marco for mass. We concelebrate mass in Italian with the priests of the Basilica around the relics of St Mark that, as the story goes, were brought here under the nose of the Turks concealed by a layer of odious pork. Walter Kenny's Italian is very good as he recites the canon in the choir stall. Following the mass we tour the square with Caterina, a very good Venetian guide. It is sad to think of the demise of the city. I believe she said that fifty percent of Venetians are over 70 years of age. We re-enter the Basilica during the 11:30 to 12:30 hour when all the domes are illuminated. The timeless gold mosaic's edges and spheres cover the same square footage, evidently, as the Maine coastline. We reassemble outside and let the sun burn off our mystical stupor and head to the glass museum. It is a bit touristy, but we buy because they know how to sell. Our final tourist event is a gondola ride. I am a veteran of travel and I have been to Venice many times before, but I never went on a gondola. At 20 euros each with a bottle of prosecco thrown in by our guide, the half hour of somnambulant ballet was well worth it. The buildings too seem to move. Mossy green steps rise out of the water between barber pole posts, chandeliers float across ceilings that ripple in watery light and the claquing of dishes and silver punctuate

July 8. 2010 Thursday.
mass @ St. Marks.
gondola.
lunch. w/ Gabriela dal Moro.
run city 1.5 hrs. 6 - 7^{30}
7:30 dinner.
9 Vivaldi Concert.
10:45 gin + tonic w/ joe + Company
on wharf.

fisherman catches small fish off the dock in Murano.
12:04. July 9. 2010

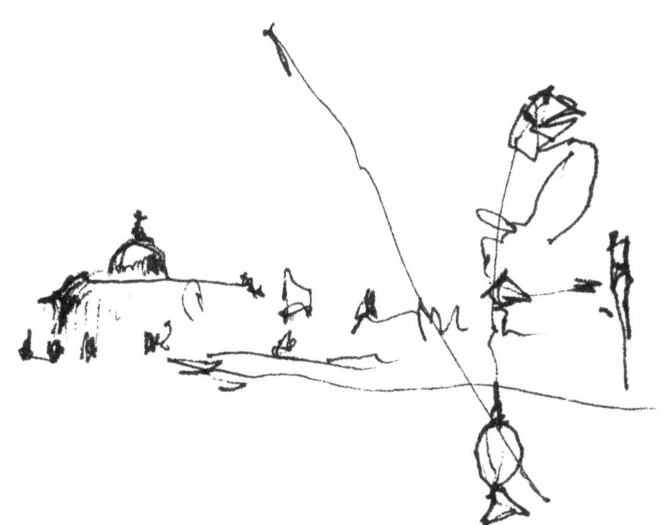

the muffled conversation over the midday meals that increase our hunger as we drift by. Gabriele leads us to a nearby sanctuary of a restaurant run by brothers from Abruzzi and they bring *antipasto* of fish and roe, fresh pasta and a caramelized compote of apricot and peach served in a table side flambé over *gelato.* Afterwards I am thinking that if I ever ran for president I would run on the siesta party.

My siesta is not long. I take a jog through the city, starting with the new Santiago Calatrava bridge by the train station. I meander through the Jewish ghetto. Its alleys are narrower than other parts of the city and stainless steel gates are hung on walls to presumably be locked over a portal to block the path of a riot or some other precaution. My goal is finding *Fondamente Nuove,* the boat stop for Torcello. We have learned there is to be a one day *sciopero,* or strike, declared this evening for tomorrow for all transit in the city. I want to go to Torcello, the original island of Venice with a legendary Cathedral on it. The total area of Venice could probably fit below Wall Street. Torcello would be like sailing to Coney Island from Water Street. We would need to walk to *Fondamente Nuove* from *Zattere* without any local boats running. Supposedly there is emergency service to the islands in the Lagoon.

After dinner four of us cross back over the Accademia Bridge and sit in the church of San Vidal for Vivaldi's *Four Seasons* played on traditional instruments. Not bad for a parish priest using what he had to work with.

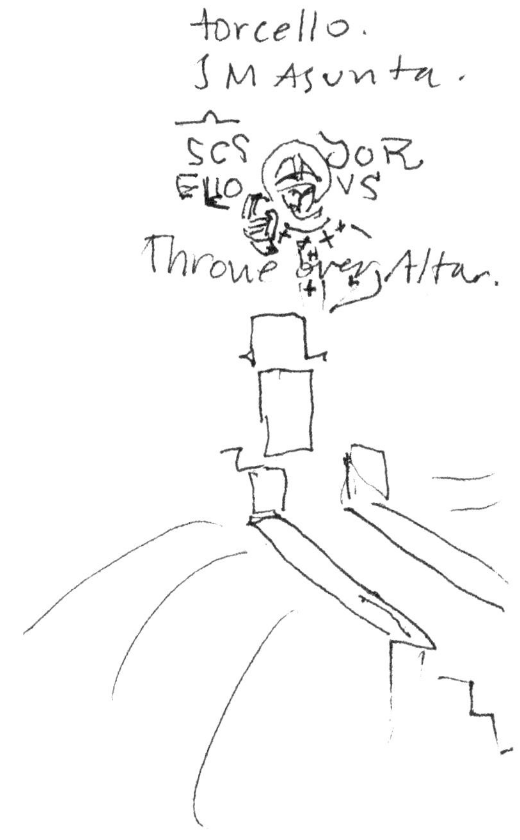

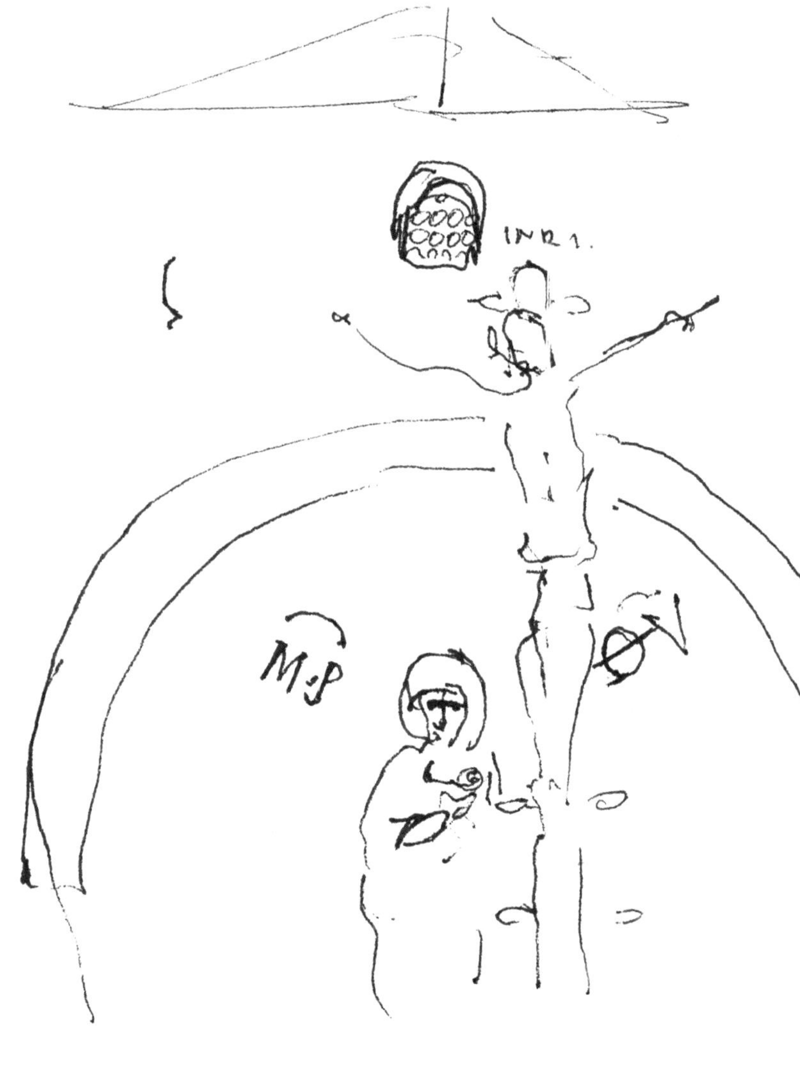
INRI.

July 9th, Friday. Venice

Following mass Artie Mastrolia and Joe Fallon offer to accompany me to Torcello. In a half hour we have walked at a comfortable pace over to *Fondamente Nuove.* The wait for a boat is long and Joe is discouraged and heads off. Artie and I take the boat that comes along to Murano, the island of the glass factory. We have time to walk and have a *cappucino* and buy some beads. Italians understandably frown on drinking a rich *cappucino* after 10 am, but considering the stress of waiting and rushing, it hits the spot. The LN boat comes in just after noon. Almost all the occupants are hopeful tourists. We creep our way through the islands hoping we will be able to get back. The towers of Mazzorbo and Burano grow, colorful fishing villages where lace is made. The Lagoon is washed in the hazy green of the heat. Torcello is a grassy estuary. A simple but handsome wharf greets the boat and visitors. Beside it the brick walls of its single canal undulate. It is a recent construction and well made. The single path on the island is lined with a few airy restaurants. A small sacred compound opens at the end of the canal that has a baptistry, that is a round separate building used as a daily chapel, a circle of ruins from the fifth and sixth centuries and a long romanesque cathedral. It is 5 euros to enter the cathedral. It is both rough hewn and magnificent. A strong rood screen and dominant corpus obscure the single figure of Santa Maria Assunta in the apse. Except for the basilica of Sant'Agnese fuori le mura on the Via Nomentana in Rome I don't remember seeing a similar single figure in a church of this period. The mosaics are the caliber of Ravenna and you wonder why such an early extravagance in a grassy island could look like it was plopped in the middle of the Meadowlands. During the Middle Ages this island apparently was home to 300,000 souls.

The steps to the throne behind the altar look like the front steps to a brownstone in Brooklyn. The floor is a Cosmati-styled floor, almond-shaped and square bits of stone set like jewels in mortar. On the far wall is the Pantokrator as action figure, in his right hand he bears like a sword a cross resembling the rood, and in his left hand he drags a terrified-looking bishop toward martyrdom. The scene is littered with locks and keys, buckles, compasses and symbols. Another Christ figure in the next lower panel is set in a mandorla that looks like an engine producing a river of fire running through wheels and quotation-mark seraphim and winding its way to a judgment scene singeing the feet of the damned.

Artie and I unpack our reflections at a sleepy restaurant under a canopy of reeds and swallows. The wine is from the island, a white wine with a saffron hue and deeply mineralized notes. It is the wine equivalent of the surprising cathedral.

After lying down in the grass under the shadow of the cathedral for a quick rest we pray for a boat. As we walk to the wharf one has just left. In a little while a speed boat comes to discharge passengers. Some French are with us. The boatman wants 40 euro to take us over to Burano which is close enough to see the *gelato* counter. The French woman with us rightly spits out: 'ridiculous'. He pulls away and turns around by the reeds and re-approaches. 30 euro. 5 each. Well, that is worth it. We step into the old boat and the magical island recedes. On Burano we have time for *gelato*. The LN rounds the bulging walls of the church yard on Mazzorbo.

Once back in Venice there is one final visit to make: to the noble rider Bartolomeo Colleoni, the hired soldier from Bergamo in the Italian Alps who came to fight and win many wars for Venice. He bequeathed a large sum for the poor and for a statue in bronze to be placed in San Marco's Square. His wish was honored except that the city fathers, the Doges, were not going to cede any real estate in front of San Marco even to a trusted hero. The square in front of Giovanni and Paolo was chosen, the largest church in Venice and adjacent to the hospital. Andrea del Verrocchio, the master of Leonardo da Vinci, sculpted the work. It is the masterful counterpart to the antique statue of Marcus Aurelius in the Campidoglio in Rome and probably the most perfectly cast and masterful bronze of the Renaissance. The flesh of the horse twitches with movement and force. The beak

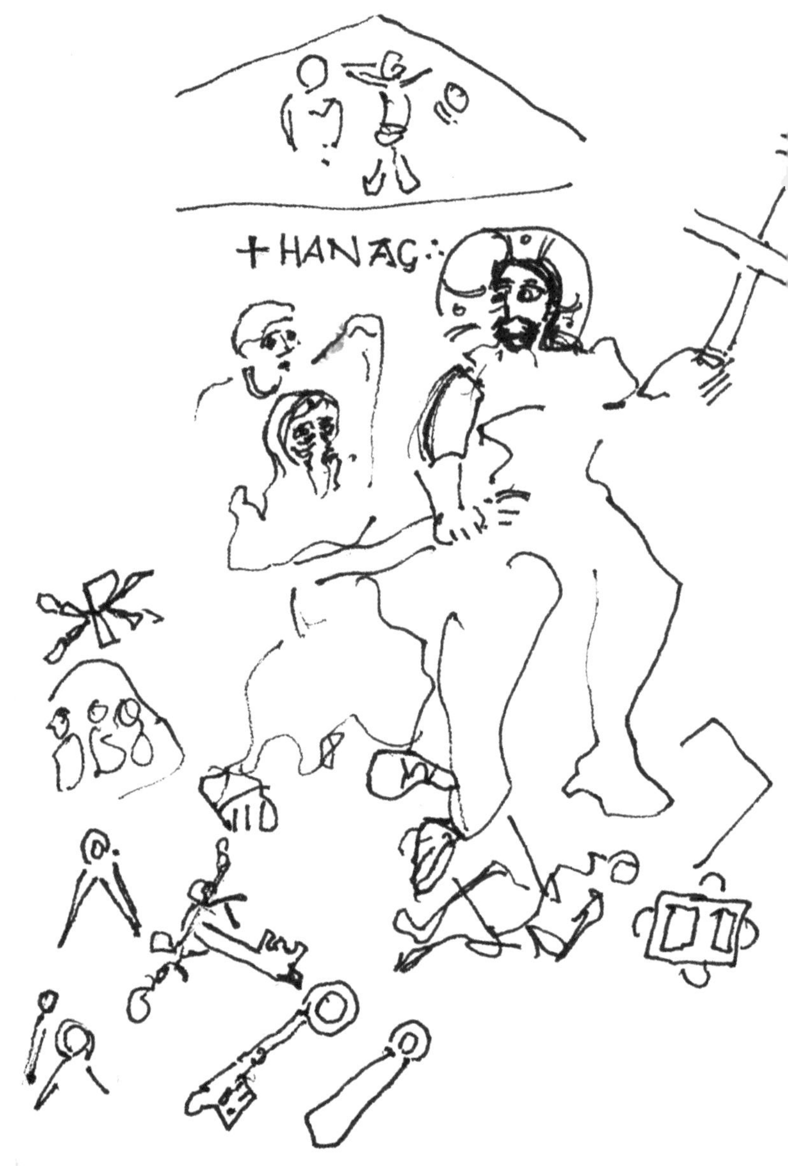
+ HANAC :

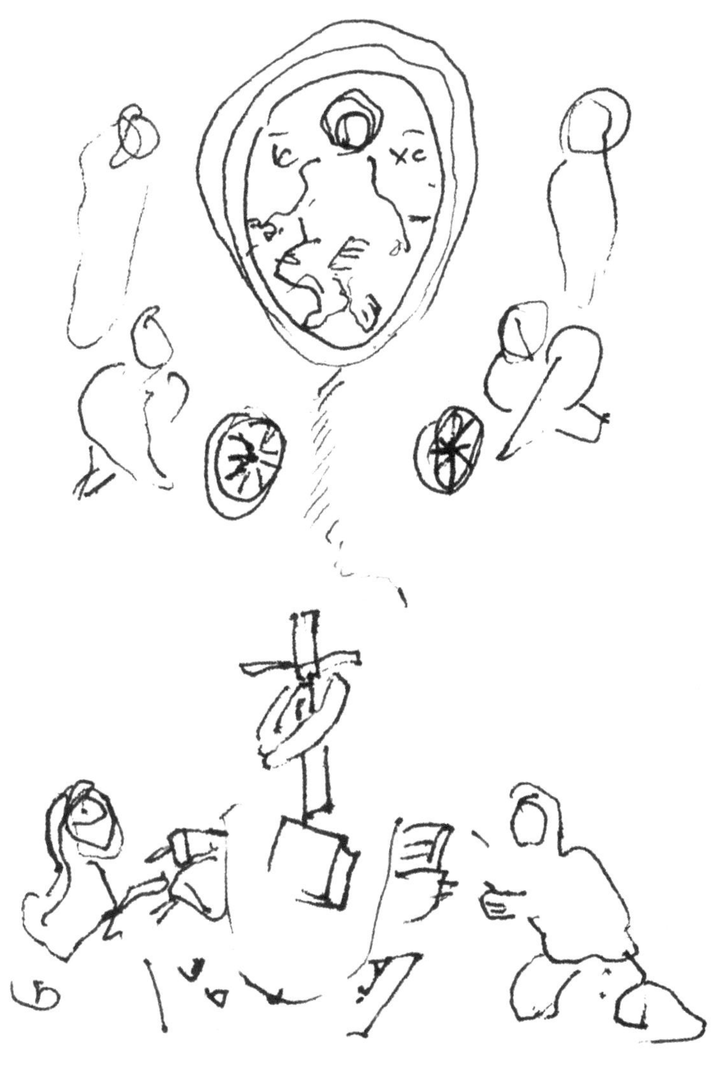
IC
XC

of the hat of the rider matches his thrusting chin. The American poet Wallace Stevens gave a famous address in Princeton in 1941 about the statue and how inspiration in art is a 'necessary angel'. Like his confrère Robert Frost did in 1947 in this seminal poem *Directive*, Stevens is on a grail-like quest to find the living waters of the artistic intuition in order to rebuild western civilization, war-torn by its mechanical rationalism. Stevens searches for the real as an achieved good, a worked-for and struggled-for goal that happens in a way that is gift, unexpected and delivered with mercy. The rider is a grateful coda to this remarkable week of study.

July 10th, Venice. Departure

We packed our bags and left them the night before for the porters and rose at 3:30 to step onto taxis. It 4:14 AM, the deadest hour. Still dark the two boats set out south to San Marco. As a tangent between San Giorgio and San Marco is crossed, we veer into the city, through the canal the engines are throttled down to a soft purr. A man hangs over laundry on a balcony and has an early morning cigarette. By the time we exit past *Fondamente Nuove* a sliver of the moon finds a watery weightlessness, and an early flush of violet and red stirs the movement of wings over the cemetery. The final run is fast in a channel marked by pilings. *Arrivederci Venezia.*

Epilogue

Alessandro Manzoni's early 19th century novel *The Betrothed* tells the story of history itself happening from the point of view of the poor. A couple engaged to be married are cruelly separated by *bravi*, the thugs of a local warlord who wants the beautiful bride for himself. At the intervention of a resourceful priest who is repenting his own past and violent response to the *bravi*, the bride, Lucia, is delivered safely to a convent and the groom, Renzo, finds himself hungry in the streets of Milan. It is during a famine. He sees stripes of flour in the street and then loaves of bread discarded and he picks one up and then another. It is the white bread he would only eat on feast days: 'It really is bread', he said aloud in amazement. 'Is this how they grow it, in a place like this, at a time like this? In a year like this? And they don't even bother picking it up when it falls? What is this, the land of plenty?' (translation Michael Moore, New York, 2022, pp. 199–200). The delight of the innocent Renzo is not misplaced. He wonders who to pay for this manna from heaven. Guidance and divine intervention are constantly interceding for them:

> Do good, Lord to those that are good,
> to the upright of heart;
> but for the crooked and those who do evil,
> Drive them away! (Psalm 125)

The story of the church is dominantly told from the top down. There are hard truths to accept. The aftermath of realignment are awkward church mergers and school closings that abandon the future. The dearth of vocations and the shrinking of the presbyterate has accelerated the flight of the faithful. These ecclesial ills reflect the greater wounds the body politic presently suffers, a society marred by mediocrity, banalized by a lack of truth, and drifting without mission. Bleak as this might seem miraculous fragments abound in Christian culture. Fragments are what was gathered after the multiplication of the loaves and fish. John includes the detail of a boy with the five loaves and the two fish. If you were a novelist you would supply details that would answer an obvious question: did no one bring any food except for one boy?

Why did the boy bring the loaves and the fish? I imagine that he was sent there by his grandmother, whom Jesus had cured in a nearby town. Unable to travel to this gathering, she gives her grandson the bread and the fish as a thanksgiving offering to Jesus himself. 'Bring this to the master. Don't drop it'. The exceptional multiplication happened as a result of a gift residing among the people and the prescient demand of Jesus to his disciples, 'Feed them yourselves'. Art arises both from what we give and from what we receive through grace; we artists labor with the fragments. The hungry crowd is still and will always be with us. After the resurrection the Risen Lord eats in front of his disciples, testifying to his physical presence, opening their minds to scripture and its transcendent truths. The miracle of the multiplication of the loaves and fish points to an unaccountable economic mystery: we do not have the energy to sustain who we are – grace provides what we lack. Abundance derives from the mystery of seed and decay – and rebirth.

Our goals as a church are not of this world, but point to an abundance that the world cannot provide. Without art in the broad sense of the word how can the eyes of faith see providence in the fall of sparrow? I am grateful for that 2010 retreat in Tuscany led by Cardinal Dolan. The fragments that I gathered then, and those I have gathered since, now fill my arms and this book, which I offer to the church in New York.

In Renaissance-era nativity scenes a ruin invariably stands in the background of the virgin and child, as in Leonardo's *Adoration of the Magi.* To me that is a powerful image of our Catholic faith in the midst of the world – decay and rebirth. Another image speaks strongly to me: the priest dropping a fragment of the host into the chalice before showing the Lamb of God to the faithful. The finite fragment both contains and points to the infinite. A church among holy ruins can expect rebirth.

Rev. Andrew More O'Connor
Utica, NY

A Modest List of Works Cited and of Works to Consider in Thinking about Art

Aristotle, *Poetics*, translation by Samuel Henry Butcher, introduction by Francis Fergusson, New York, 1961.

What do we mean by 'art'? Aristotle uses the word poetics to refer to a work of the practical intellect, which is what we are excited about when we encounter that thing called 'art'. *Poesis* is the Greek word for 'making', and this is Aristotle's concern: a making that helps us see ourselves. In the ancient world physical work was the domain of slaves and reflected a caste system. The 5th century B.C. witnessed a world-wide challenge to this system, which Karl Jaspers famously called the 'Axis of History'. Centered in the truth of the free person, Buddha, Confucius, Lao Tze, the Upanishads and the Hebrew prophets and the Greek philosophers, all developed a common moral code. Eric Vogelin in his *New Science of Politics* contends that only in the West was the challenge was the work of the city, the *polis.* He further notes the soteriological truth of the birth of a savior as the true axis of history. God must enter into the world to answer the conflict between the cosmological truth and personal freedom. Hence, in the *Poetics,* Aristotle, even without a Christian vision understands the crisis of the tragic hero as a figure of the cosmological order who endures a crisis as a result of a *hamartia,* the tragic human flaw, which we call original sin.

Jacques Barzun, *The Use and Abuse of Art.* A.W. Mellon Lectures in the Fine Arts, 1974.

A potent survey of the explorations of modern art with a philosophical groundwork for the layman to understand why, for instance, avant-garde art seeks to invalidate all previous work in a quest to be new through shock, whereas minimalist art, such as that of Mark Rothko, engages tradition. The contemporary believer often rejects modern art as all bad, not understanding that modern artists feel liberated from the figurative since the rise of photography.

Italo Calvino, *Lezioni americane. Sei proposte per il prossimo millennio,* Turin, 1988; English translation by Patrick Creagh with the title *Six memos for the next millennium,* Cambridge (MA), 1988.

These essays originated with Harvard's invitation to Calvino towards the end of his life. In it he theorizes that the muses originated from the winged hooves of Pegasus that clop and break open rocks that cap the eternal springs atop Mount Helicon as a reward to Theseus, who through the mirror of his shield, avoids being turned to stone as he cuts off the Gorgon's head and stores it. The victorious slowness and power of art to deflect the mortal wound of nature reflects its resolve.

Marie-Alain Couturier, O.P., *Art sacré,* texts selected by Dominique de Menil and Pie Duployé, Houston, 1983; English translation by Granger Ryan Austin–Houston, 1989.

Father Couturier was a Catholic priest, art critic, and famed designer of stained glass. He devoted a good part of his life to a responding to Le Corbusier, who in 1935 chastised the Catholic Church for abandoning its role as guardian of the arts. He did so by cultivating a dialogue with Matisse that led to his mid-century masterpiece *Chapelle du Rosaire* in Vence, France. *Art sacré* concerns the intersection between the roles of art with the soul and spirituality, especially the important roles of poverty and form.

Loren C. Eiseley, *Man, Time and Prophecy*, San Diego, 1966.

My father introduced me to Eiseley, in 1980 with his volume of poems *Notes of an Alchemist*. In a bookshop in New Haven I discovered his *Man, Time and Prophecy*, his address to the centennial class of the University of Kansas. This slim volume is written by this poet/anthropologist/geologist who referred to himself as a 'chresmologue', which he defines as an 'ancient dealer in crumbling parchment and uncertain prophecy'. Some of the seminarians at Dunwoodie during my years there (1990–6) were from Nebraska as was Eiseley. We read this aloud and it taught us what prophecy sounds like.

Robert Frost, *Collected Poems, Prose and Plays*, edited by Richard Poirier and Mark Richardson, New York, 1995.

For Catholics Frost is especially significant as one whose imagination transcended his inherited puritan worldview. Especially important is his post-war poem *Directive*, that I quoted in *A Tuscan Résumé*. *Directive* honors the recovery within the ruins of our culture of the holy grail, a broken goblet, which for Frost was under a 'spell', so the 'wrong ones don't get in and get saved'.

Seamus Heaney, *The Redress of Poetry*, New York, 1995.

Seamus Heaney signed his first poems in Latin *Incertus*, uncertain, because he was a Catholic writing in and about the North during the Troubles, but also because he was searching for that immovable point in which to build a political language of stability and peace. I stumbled into him at a vocational moment when I wandered into Sligo, Ireland during the Yeats Summer Festival in 1981. He was 42 and I was 18. I have studied him ever since and understand his discipline as locating the immovable point upon which Heraclitus's fulcrum is poised to move the world: in the poetic act. *Incertus* reflected his uncertain role as the voice of the dispossessed in the North. This volume of essays, one of many, established for me the profound truth that this dispossession was a blessing under the cloak of a curse.

Milan Kundera, *L'Art du roman*, Paris 1986; English translation by Linda Asher, Boston, 1993.

Franz Kafka lived in the wall of Prague's Castle. Kundera, famous for being the voice of the gentle revolt against the communist regime of Cold War-era Czechoslovakia in his novel the *Unbearable Lightness of Being*, considers in this work the form of the novel through Kafka's response to the assault on the self.

William F. Lynch, S.J., *Christ and Apollo. The Dimensions of the Literary Imagination*, Notre Dame–London, 1975 (new ed.; 1st ed. New York, 1960).

Father Lynch approaches the balancing act that art makes in describing the truth. He uses the terms 'univocal' and 'equivocal' to state the extremes: either one thing is true (univocal) and that one thing defines all things (he was thinking of totalitarian reductionism), or the opposite (equivocal) all things are true equally. Both are pernicious. Apollonian thinking represents these extremes and Christ, in contrast, the 'interpenetration of opposites'.

Jacques Maritain, *Creative Intuition in Art and Poetry*, New York, 1953; repr. Princeton (NJ), 1981.

Maritain rejects the popular association of art with the irrational. Instead Maritain explores the 'suprarational' logic of art which he locates in the 'musical unconscious'. He deals in this way with the communal mystery of art. This volume prompts us to ask the question: why do we all intimate the meaning of art to be greater than any one particular rendering?

Alessandro Manzoni, *I promessi sposi* [1840–2], English translation by Michael Moore with the title *The Betrothed*, New York, 2022.

Manzoni returns from France to his native Lecco, Italy, disillusioned by French atheism. He rediscovers his Catholic faith and creates a new form for the novel, told from the point of view of the poor. Pope Francis strongly encourages everyone, especially engaged couples, to read this delightful novel.

Thomas Merton, 'The Vatican Council and Sacred Art', essay from 1964 (available at merton.org).

Father Merton, a Trappist monk, reminds us that sacred art is by definition depicting an image. It cannot be about nothing. It must depict something. Merton understands the usefulness of modern abstract art. Doing so leads to the joy of discovering color and shape without the noise of too much detail. Nonetheless, Merton understands the need for Catholic artists to depict images; the angel appears before Mary. The struggle in each era to depict this incarnational reality is exciting and necessary.

Monasticism and the Arts. edited by Timothy Verdon, with the assistance of John Dally, foreword by John W. Cook, Syracuse (NY), 1984.

The concept of *Theoria*, thinking about God with the realizable hope of seeing him, of representing him and of not being swallowed into the infinity of God, makes this volume of the collective reflections on the tradition of art and the monastic movements of the church over the centuries so compelling. This volume originated in a symposium moderated by Monsignor Verdon. I attended a portion of this symposium when I was a high school student in New Haven.

Wallace Stevens, *The Necessary Angel, Essays on Reality and The Imagination*, New York, 1951.

For Stevens art reflects the metaphysical hierarchies which we mere human beings were made to wrestle with.

Allen Tate, 'The Symbolic Imagination', in *Essays of Four Decades*, Chicago, 1968; new ed. 1999.

In this famous essay he defines the Christian imagination as not 'angelic' – an evil word in his vocabulary indicating thought without a body – but rather 'symbolic'. Tate uses the example of St Catherine's promise to catch the head of a repentant criminal. She had the imaginative capacity to accept both the reality of the human blood and that of the Blood of the Lamb. I studied with of one of his students, Dr. Louise Cowan. Tate once said, 'you can live without poetry but you cannot live well'.

Selected Papal Documents Reflecting on Art and Catholic Imagination

Pope Paul VI, 'The Artists' Mass', Sistine Chapel, May 7, 1964.

Pope Paul VI began the tradition of addressing modern artists in the Sistine Chapel. His comments explore the common fate that religion and art suffer in the modern world: being relegated to the trash heap of the superfluous in human history. Paul VI introduces the theme of the loss of the transcendent – a theme that he and subsequent popes continue to elaborate on.

Pope John Paul II, 'Letter to Artists', Sistine Chapel, Easter Sunday, April 4, 1999.

Comprehensive philosophical, historical and theological rendering of art in which 'both heaven and earth have a hand'.

Pope Benedict XVI, 'Letter to Artists', Sistine Chapel, November 21, 2009.

Address with humble reference to JPII's call to artists to cultivate epiphanies to accompany and help guide man to salvation.

Pope Francis, 'Address of His Holiness Pope Francis to Artists for the 50th Anniversary of the Inauguration of the Vatican Museums' Collection of Modern Art', June 23, 2023.

Sistine Chapel address in which Pope Francis likens art to a child's recognition that the essence of his being is oriented toward life and not death.

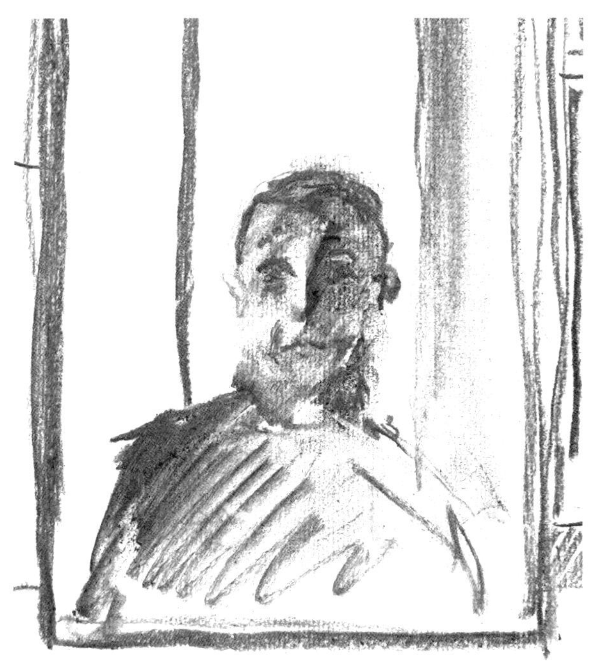

Self-portrait

Rev. Andrew More O'Connor
is a priest of the Archdiocese of New York and an artist.
For more information on his art and to contact him:

www.sacredartheals.com

July 2024

Printed by Grafiche Martinelli, Bagno a Ripoli (Florence)
Bound by Legatoria Firenze